GILDED SONGS
(Berlin through Bacharach)

THE GIG INSTRUMENTALIST'S GUIDE
TO THE

Songs of the Golden Era of
American Popular Song
(1920 to 1979)

A perspective

by

Michael G. Cunningham

AuthorHouse™
1663 Liberty Drive
Bloomington, IN 47403
www.authorhouse.com
Phone: 1-800-839-8640

First published by AuthorHouse 09/03/2010

ISBN: 978-1-4520-4527-6 (sc)
ISBN: 978-1-4520-4528-3 (e)

Library of Congress Control Number: 2010911784

Printed in the United States of America
Bloomington, Indiana

This book is printed on acid-free paper.

PREFACE

This book is the result of the author spending a lifetime playing by ear perhaps 65% of the songs listed. Between 1959 and 1969 he was an intensely involved professional pianist, indulging in an avid love of this repertory. As time passed he received college music degrees, including a Doctorate in Music Composition from Indiana University. He also taught a university course in the 1980s which led to efforts to make further sense of an obviously fascinating era that had ended. Informal research and discovery then invited publication. There has always been a need for books like this, and the Alec Wilder's (*American Popular Song*, 1972) was certainly a good start. But, differing from the Wilder in a number of ways, and from of other writings, this book attempts specific composer ranking and focuses on a wider range of the best of the songs. There are also other differences that become obvious.

Gig musicians, while being able to play many of these songs from memory, are frequently in the dark as to the composer, lyricist and time period of origin. This problem has also been compounded by the universal tendency to associate songs with their performers, and not the creators. And when one focuses on the actual song composers, further problems are presented by the existence of two rival performance rights organizations, ASCAP, and BMI, one would always resort to directories of songs their composer members, and the other seemingly less interested in such books.

Since this book is aimed at gig musicians, as opposed to gig singers, songs in this perspective are treated as pieces of music, not textual messages. (The needs of singers are different, and would require a different sort of book.) By focusing on the music, consistency and a greater simplicity of presentation is made possible. Otherwise the whole era remains a nearly impenetrable quagmire of equalized data. This perspective is therefore Composer/Music biased, but without in any way denigrating the importance of lyrics. During this period, all too often there were instances of failed songs with excellent lyrics but ineffective music. Conversely, songs with merely passable lyrics and effective music were often successful. And obviously, the composers were not all equal. So, throughout the first part of the book up to 1960, and to the extent that is possible in the '60s and '70s, composers are ranked. There is also an attempt to draw attention to the many instances of fine songs coming from composers who only had one or two successes. The author also believes in the beautiful, but earlier unrecognized beautiful song that waits for discovery.

There is no attempt to cover all subcategories of popular music during the period discussed. For instance, there is little mention of what later became known as Country-Western music. Nor will much be said or indicated concerning the Rock period that overlapped, beginning in the 1950s. These and other subcategories will remain for other more qualified writers to address. Rather, this book deals with songs that were popular in the Eastern Urban culture, songs that seemingly dominated mass media as it then existed.

The author here assumes the daunting task of presuming to be a nation's musical memory. To the author's knowledge, this kind of book and its particular slant has never been attempted. Therefore choices and evaluations had to be made in the interest of perspective and purely musical content and quality. Many highly popular songs were thus omitted, usually because their catchy, and often excellent lyrics were their only saving grace. As was hinted at above, a measure of just why songs are included in this book would be the gifted musician's ability to play them from memory, harmony included. While that may seem a strange criterion to some, musicians who function mainly "by ear" have been around since the very beginnings of music, and what they can and cannot memorize with ease matters. The harmonic aspect of the majority the songs here is somehow related to the way chords move in most of the music since the days of J. S. Bach, and that assists in their memorization.

It remains a problem for anyone to define a bad song from a musical standpoint. Perhaps there are two kinds: the first would obviously be amateurishly constructed, and the second would be the kind this book additionally avoids: the bland type. A bland song does not stay in the memory. (Every composer from the past has unintentionally created bland pieces.) Musically bland songs do things correctly, not memorably, and fade into a musically statistical blur.

TABLE OF CONTENTS

INTRODUCTION

This is not a history of popular song, although some may find it assists in that sense. It is not about the personal lives of the song creators, nor about shows or movies. Such information can be found in other authors' writings, and is here almost irrelevant. Here the composers are spoken of in terms of their work. Moreover, there is no attempt to completely list all the songs that were popular. Rather quality is sought over popularity. References to jazz are kept to a minimum. However, certain songs that were/are overwhelmingly associated with Jazz performance are indicated.

For the period under discussion, what is a good song? It is not necessarily one that earned much money. Rather it is one that has a unique and easily remembered melody, a well-constructed harmonic plan, and most of the time either a bifid form (ABAC), or a ballad form (AABA). The overwhelming majority of the songs listed here are constructed quadratically, in that four phrases of eight measures each most frequently add up to a 32 measures length song. There might be extensions at the close, but the quadratic impression is clear. This formal template was common to most of the songs of the era, and aided in memorization, and most assuredly provided guidelines to those wishing to compose songs. The harmonic plans were usually very plain, functional and definitely linked in with the Rameau/Bach harmony from History, so as to appeal to the musically less experienced for easier comprehension and extra sales. (The Golden Era was mainly one of piano sheet sales.) Professional performers and arrangers, in turn, would usually enliven the rhythm and vary the plainness of the harmony with extra color notes and equivalent and/or substitute chords. And usually arrangers and performers were careful in not changing the given melody too much. (Unlike many singers singing Golden Era songs in the following era.)

In this book, composer names usually come before that of the lyricists. For those who place too great an emphasis on lyrics, it is interesting to note that, while Cole Porter was an excellent lyricist of all his many songs, only a small proportion of them became enduring classics, and it was not just by chance. It is the music which potentially gives songs long-lasting power. And so, the songs listed in this book easily stand on their own without the need singers or lyrics. While it is natural that the accepted titles of songs are used, it is ironic that gig instrumentalists who play from memory, in a very primal way, regard the first few notes of the melody as the musical title. Since most of the time they live in a world of musical communication without words, titles are indeed music itself. This book is aimed at such musicians.

Also here we are usually dealing with a pre-1970 Eastern Urban popular music that seemingly dominated radio, recordings and television. These songs appealed to a mostly middle-class urban population. The whole conditioning process and the music industry may well have been highly influenced by the Society of Composers, Authors and Publishers (ASCAP, founded in 1914), an organization of songwriters that (until the 1940s) almost completely controlled what the public heard on mass media. This organization not only insured that songwriters would make money from high profile performances of their songs, but for a while it also controlled the musical quality and maturity of the songs. But, this being America, with its value of the little entrepreneur-guy, there would eventually be "music industry" people who would make much money catering to a wider common denominator of the population. So, the floodgates of novelty, and an increasingly temporary popularity were opened up. Added to this, by the mid 1950s the new post WWII generation (with much money to spend) was targeted with an almost throwaway immature kind of song. So the very high quality spoken of in this book became a moot point in the face of such popularity and high profits. But for this book, that measurement of high quality still stands.

Here we deal with the Golden Era, that "song Camelot" period that graced and seemingly dominated our culture for a brief while. These songs frequently exhibited unusual harmonizations, seventh and chromatic chords and attractive modulations. And if the songs themselves didn't have those three elements, arrangers and stylists would do all they could to include them. This period produced a highly memorable repertory that today, while existing just beneath the surface of mass media, doesn't seem to go away. Maybe that justifies the "Classic" label that is so frequently used.

It may be that the 1930s were the center of gravity of the entire Golden era, because that decade stands out for its extremely high quality songs produced by composers who seemingly produced only one note-worthy song. It had to have been Radio, and the proliferation of sound movies that brought this about. The mostly urban population, along with budding song composers were learning fast.

Please forgive if some deserving composer or song has been omitted or slighted. To the author, gems continue to appear, even as of this writing. Also, a few not-too-famous songs, a few songs of the newer era, and (unfortunately) a few bland songs, may have accidentally crept in because of certain organization reasons, or because they seem to help make a point.

The 20ᵗʰ Century's aughts and teens:

OPERETTA

Until the 1950s, there seemed to be a significant audience for operetta productions and singers. The biggest money earners on Broadway were often operettas. (Take away the lyrics from the songs of Frederick Loewe, and what remains is operetta music.) While this kind of popular music, with its many waltzes, seemed at odds with Golden Era music, it turned out that, if this genre was not safe as a money making style, neither were the songs of the Golden Era. So, ironically, the demise in popularity of operetta in the late 1950s signaled the demise of the Golden Era not too many years later. Thus the listed songs here would cease being "major market." In retrospect, perhaps there was some unusual symbiotic relationship between the two styles.

Of the operetta songs listed in this book, little will be said concerning their style. While many of them have profoundly beautiful melodies, they lose their character without staid basic triadic harmony. (In Music Theory parlance, I-IV-V-I). Contrarily, Golden-era songs were more easily adapted to alternate and substitute harmonizations. Very few of the operetta songs were given a jazz treatment. Only one readily comes to mind, and it is Romberg's "Lover, Come Back to Me." It may be that the thought of operetta so turned off jazz performers that they usually passed up likely possibilities. Still, for today's world, many of the most popular operetta songs are outright waltzes that remain easily memorized. There may even be an occasional request for one of these pieces in the 21ˢᵗ century.

The most important operetta composers in the U. S. were Victor Herbert, Rudolph Friml, Noel Coward, and Sigmund Romberg. Each of these composers, while having occasional stage flops, earned much money from their stage successes and attendant songs.

Victor Herbert (1859 to 1924)
The Victor Herbert songs, sweet though they are, seemed to have passed into history. Television broadcasts of classic movies still keep some alive.

HERBERT'S surviving songs:
Ah! Sweet Mystery of Life
Gypsy Love Song
I'm falling in Love With Someone
Indian Summer (1940s pop song derived from his Cello Sonata)
Italian Street Song
Kiss in the Dark, A
Kiss Me Again
March of the Toys
Neapolitan Love Song
Streets of New York, The
Sweethearts
Thine Alone
Toyland
Tramp, Tramp, Tramp
When You're Away

Herbert worked with a number of lyricists, most of whom eventually lost fame. The most prominent of them was probably Buddy DeSylva, who later headed Paramount Pictures in the early 1940s.

Rudolph Friml (1879 to 1972)
Friml's surviving famous songs are smaller in number, and his success resulted from a very few blockbuster stage productions that were also later filmed.

FRIML'S surviving songs:
Donkey Serenade, The
Giannina Mia
Indian Love Call
L'amour, Toujours, L'amour
Only a Rose
Rose Marie
Some Day
Of the American lyricists who worked with him, Otto Harbach and Oscar Hammerstein II are the most famous.

British Noel Coward (1899 to 1973)
Coward was a theatrical genius who could do it all, creating his own stage scripts and lyrics. As a composer he could also occasionally create top-notch operetta songs.   Some stage commentators have referred to him as the British Cole Porter, but surely that refers only to the clever quality of his lyrics. The following list is short but potent. Four of them are clearly operetta waltzes.

COWARD SONGS
I'll Follow My Secret Heart
I'll See You Again
Mad About the Boy
Mad Dogs and Englishmen go out in the mid-day sun.
Someday I'll Find You
Ziguener (a Gypsy song)

Sigmund Romberg (1887 to 1951)
The last of this group of operetta composers was of a later generation, with a high public profile as late as the mid 1950s. He was also probably the most successful of those listed here. As was mentioned above, at least one of his songs* was/is often used by jazz performers.

ROMBERG SONGS
Close as Pages in a Book
Deep in my Heart
Desert Song, The
Drinking Song, The
Golden Days
Lost in Loveliness
Lover, Come Back to Me * JAZZ FAVORITE
One Alone
One Kiss
Riff Song, The
Romance
Serenade
Silver Moon
Softly, As in a Morning Sunrise
Stouthearted Men
Wanting You
When I Grow Too Old to Dream
Will You Remember? (Sweethearts)

Among his various lyricists the most famous are Otto Harbach, Oscar Hammerstein II, Leo Robin and Dorothy Fields.

BROADWAY AND TIN PAN ALLEY SONGS CONTEMPORENOUS WITH THE HIGHLY INTENSE OPERETTA PERIOD (Including WWI years)

Other sources of popular songs that preceded the Golden Era, are the Broadway Theater, Vaudeville theaters nationwide, and their "song feeder" source, the early Manhattan song publishing trade (located in a few lower Manhattan buildings) known as Tin Pan Alley. Song fame can deteriorate over time, and any song survival list is arguable. With that proviso in mind, the following songs are perhaps the most popular over the greater part of the 20th Century. Certainly each of the following composers produced many more songs than the lists would imply.

George Michael Cohan (1878 to 1942)

The songs of this Broadway legendary figure (the only person with a statue on Broadway) date from approximately 1900 to 1920. Apparently he was his own lyricist.

Give My Regards to Broadway
Harrigan
Mary's a Grand Old Name
Over There
Yankee Doodle Boy
You're a Grand Old Flag

Ernest R. Ball (1878 to 1927)

(working with various lyricists)
Dear Little Boy of Mine
Let the Rest of the World Go By
Little Bit of Heaven, A
Mother Macree
When Irish Eyes are Smiling

Harry von Tilzer (1872 to 1946)

(Various lyricists)
Bird in a Gilded Cage, A
I Want a Girl
On a Sunday Afternoon
Under the Anheuser Bush
Wait Till the Sun Shines, Nellie
When My Baby Smiles at Me

Albert von Tilzer (1878 to 1956)

(Lew Brown is his most famous lyricist.)
I'll Be With You in Apple Blossom Time
I'm the Lonesomest Gal in Town
My Little Girl
Oh, By Jingo
Put Your Arms Around Me, Honey
Take Me Out to the Ball Game

Fred Fisher (1875 to 1942)

(Billy Rose is his most famous lyricist.)
Chicago
Come, Josephine, in my Flying Machine
Dardanella
Peg O' My Heart

Added to the above are many songs from composers who had only one or two hits. It is a potent list. It may be that most composers here were capable of only one or two good and lasting songs.

INDEPENDENT SONGS 1910 to 1913:

After the Ball by Charles K. Harris
Anchors Aweigh by Charles A. Zimmerman, R. Lovell, Al H. Miles
Because by Guy D'Hardelot and Edward Teschemacher
Bill Bailey, Won't you Please Come Home by Hughie Cannon
By the Light of the Silvery Moon by Gus Edwards and Edward Madden
Chinatown, My Chinatown by Jean Schwartz and William Jerome
Cuddle Up a Little Closer by Karl Hoschna and Otto Harbach
Daisy Bell by Harry Dacre
Down By the Old Mill Stream by Tell Taylor and Earl K. Smith
Every Little Movement by Karl Hoschna and Otto Harbach
I Love You Truly by Carrie Jacobs Bond.
I Wonder Who's Kissing Her Now by J. E. Howard. F. R. Adams and W. M. Hough
In My Merry Oldsmobile by Gus Edwards and Vincent Brian
In the Shade of the Old Apple Tree by Egbert Van Alstyne and Harry H. Williams
It's a Long, Long Way to Tipperary by Jack Judge and Harry Williams
Let Me Call You Sweetheart by Leo Friedman and Beth Whitson
Meet Me in St. Louis, Louis by Kerry Mills and Andrew B. Sterling
Meet Me Tonight in Dreamland by Leo Friedman and Beth Whitson
Moonlight Bay by Percy Wenrich and Edward Madden
My Melancholy Baby by Ernie Burnett and George A. Norton
My Wild Irish Rose by Chancey Olcott
National Emblem by E. E. Bagley
Oh, You Beautiful Doll by Nat D. Ayer and A. Seymour Brown
On the road to Mandalay by Oley Speaks and Rudyard Kipling and
On Wisconsin by W. T. Purdy and Carl Beck
Put On Your Old Grey Bonnet by Percy Wenrich and Stanley Murphy
Ragtime Cowboy Joe by M. Abrahams, G. Clark and L. F. Muir
School Days by Gus Edwards and Will D. Cobb
Shine On, Harvest Moon by Nora Bayes and Jack Norworth
Sidewalks of New York by James W. Blake and Charles B. Lawler
Some of These Days by Shelton Brooks
Sweet Adeline by Harry Armstrong and Richard H. Gerard
Sweetheart of Sigma Chi, The by F. Dudleigh Vernor and Byron D. Stokes
That's a Plenty by Bert A. Williams and Henry Creamer (Lew Pollack)
Too-Ra-Loo-Ra-Loo-Ral, That's an Irish Lullaby by James Royce Shannon
Trail of the Lonesome Pine, The by Harry Carroll and Ballard MacDonald
Waiting for the Robert E. Lee by Louis F. Muir and L. Wolfe Gilbert
Whiffenpoof Song, The by T. Galloway, M. Minnigerode, G. Pomeroy

1914 to 1919:

Aba Daba Honeymoon by Walter Donovan and Arthur Fields
After You've Gone by Henry Creamer and Turner Layton
Alice Blue Gown by Harry Tierney and Joseph McCarthy
Baby, Won't You Please Come Home? by Charles Warfield and Clarence Williams
Beautiful Ohio by Mary Earl and Ballard MacDonald
Bells of St. Mary's, The by A. Emmet Adams and Douglas Furber
By the Beautiful Sea by Harry Carroll and Harold Atterridge
Darktown Strutter's Ball by Shelton Brooks
Down Among the Sheltering Palms by Abe Olman and James Brockman
For Me and My Gal by George W. Meyer, Edgar Leslie and Ray Goetz
Good Man is Hard to Find, A by Eddie Green
Hindustan by Oliver G. Wallace and Harold Weeks
I'm Always Chasing Rainbows by F. Chopin, Harry Carroll and Joseph McCarthy
I'm Forever Blowing Bubbles by John W. Kellette and Jean Kenbrovin
If You Were the Only Girl In the World by Nat D. Ayer and Clifford Grey
Ja-Da by Bob Carleton
Jelly Roll Blues by Fred Morton
Johnson Rag, The by Guy Hall and Henry Kleinauf
K-K-K-Katy by Geoffrey O'Hara
Memories by Egbert Van Alstyne and Gus Kahn
Missouri Waltz, The by Frederich Logan and James R. Shannon
Oh Johnny, Oh Johnny, Oh! By Abe Olman and Ed Rose
Pack Up Your Troubles in Your Old Kit-Bag by Felix Powell and George Asaf
Poor Butterfly by Raymond Hubbell and John L. Golden --- SWING FAVORITE
Pretty Baby by E. Van Alstyne, T. Jackson and Gus Kahn
Rock-a-Bye Your Baby With a Dixie Melody by Jean Schwartz, Sam Lewis, and Joe Young
Rose of Washington Square by James F. Hanley and Ballard MacDonald
Roses of Picardy by Haydn Wood, and Frederick E. Weatherly
Smiles by Lee G. Roberts and J. Will Callahan
Smilin' Through by Arthur A. Penn
Somebody Stole My Gal by Leo Wood
St. Louis Blues by W. C. Handy
Sugar Blues by Clarence Williams and Lucy Fletcher
There's a Long, Long Trail by Zo Elliot and Stoddard King
Tiger Rag by the Original Dixie Jazz Band and Harry De Costa
Twelfth Street Rag by Euday L. Bowman
When You Wore a Tulip by Percy Wenrich and Jack Mahoney
World is Waiting for the Sunshine, The by Ernest Seitz and Eugene Lockhart

----

During this first part of the 20th Century there are also a number of highly popular marches by John Phillip Sousa.

THE FIRST RANK OF COMPOSERS-The Big Five
CONSISTING OF JEROME KERN, IRVING BERLIN, RICHARD RODGERS, GEORGE GERSHWIN AND COLE PORTER

_____

JEROME KERN   (1885 to 1945)

Jerome Kern's songs frequently exhibit profoundly charming melodic skill, as well as (in his final decades) brief and bold modulations. His melodies can sometimes soar into high and low realms because he wrote for professional voices with wide range. But large range, as such, was not the goal. Rather, it was always in the pursuit of melodic grace. All of these traits were usually even more evident during his last six years. (The poor quality of songs used in the 1940 film, ONE NIGHT IN THE TROPICS, probably are the result of an ill man, not having quite recovered from a stroke.) If there was a weakness, or rather a telltale indication that Kern came from an earlier era, it was his rhythm. For him an adventurous rhythm was what he had heard during the minstrel and ragtime eras. Any of the newer rhythms after 1930 were merely added by then current performers and arrangers.

Kern was for a number of decades seen as the most important popular song composer of the Golden Era, and there is a good case for his being accorded that honor. Hard though it may be to believe, and by certain accounts, Kern envied operetta composer Sigmund Romberg. Kern may have been acclaimed as top man, but he had singled out another figure whose successes egged him on. Kern, even with all the respect he enjoyed, could be rather high-handed. One sometimes comes across highly unfavorable comments concerning his reputation in Show Business, and in particular during preparations for an opening show. Kern's lyricists had a special problem in dealing with his songs. Their challenge was to find the right words that would not interfere with the melody's original version. Still, they managed. Indeed, there are some late songs that involve more than one (famous) lyricist, and it may well have been to find just the right word or clause that would not interfere with Kern's original melody.

Later in Kern's life, his imaginative modulations were carefully crafted. According to one famous lyricist, he would sometimes struggle at the piano to make certain transitions in and out of certain keys work smoothly. Later jazz pianists and arrangers would have a field day working with his songs, often using equivalent and substitute chords, along with new swing, and later, more complex jazz rhythms. Additionally, since the Golden Era ran simultaneously with the ascendance and dominance of many pop singers, of whom Bing Crosby and Frank Sinatra were at the lead, Kern, Kern and all of his fellow composers had to endure rarely hearing their melodies as they had written them. Supposedly Kern abhorred the swing/jazz rhythms and freer melodic treatments, but chose to do little about it because of huge ASCAP performance and replay royalties from Radio, Movies and phonograph recordings. (Many a songwriter was silenced by constant mass-media performances and the resulting royalty profits.)

It is surprising that at the beginning of the 21st Century, Kern's fame had diminished among the ever new generations. At the turn of the 21st Century, Irving Berlin was frequently being cited as the great wonder, probably because of longevity and catchy lyrics that appealed to a wider population. But back in Kern's day, that was certainly not the perception. It was Richard Rodgers, who in saluting Kern in a published memorial booklet, ranked him as highest in the field. Apparently, Kern's craft at melody and accompaniment kept Rodgers' dream alive. Other contemporaneous figures in the business also knew that Kern was the top man. Later figures, such as the eminent Leonard Bernstein, later in the 20th century cited Kern as a rare melodist. Certainly Kern lived at a time when beautiful melody mattered. Indeed the quality of his songs had made him seem ineffable. When he died suddenly in late 1945, there were nation-wide radio tributes, something that has not happened for any other composer since. One particular broadcast is preserved today on a commercial recording.

KERN SONGS
All the Things You Are – JAZZ FAVORITE
All Through the Day
Bill

Can't Help Lovin' That Man
Can't Help Singing
Dearly Beloved -- JAZZ FAVORITE
Fine Romance, A
Folks Who Live on the Hill, The
I Dream Too Much
I Won't Dance
I'm Old Fashioned
I've Told Every Little Star
In Love in Vain
Last Time I Saw Paris, The
Long Ago and Far Away
Look For the Silver Lining
Lovely to Look At
Make Believe
More and More
Night Was Made for Love, The
Ol' Man River
Pick Yourself Up – JAZZ FAVORITE
She Didn't Say Yes
Smoke Gets in Your Eyes
Song is You, The -- JAZZ FAVORITE
Sunny
They Didn't Believe Me
Till the Clouds Roll By
Touch of Your Hand, The
Way You Look Tonight, The   -- JAZZ FAVORITE
Who?
Why Do I Love You?
Why Was I Born?
Yesterdays
You Are Love
You Were Never Lovelier
You're Devastating

Kern's most famous lyricists were P. G. Wodehouse, Oscar Hammerstein II, Otto Harbach, Johnny Mercer, E. Y. (Yip) Harburg, Dorothy Fields, and Ira Gershwin.

IRVING BERLIN (1888 to 1989)

He was his own lyricist. In terms of style, there were two Irving Berlins. One, the Market-Place Berlin, was the enormously successful composer of popular songs that reflected aspects of every day life. His were songs that could be simple and sentimental, use peppy syncopations, and use colloquial textual expressions that were part of the ordinary man's daily life. More correctly, they are expressions that could be heard in the New York of his day. This is the Berlin who regarded a good song as one that earned money, and a bad song was otherwise.   This is the Berlin who would recycle parts of unsuccessful songs into newer songs. An example would be the bridge of "The Yam" being recycled some 15 years later into "Count Your Blessings."   A more famous example is the melody of "Easter Parade" being recycled with newer lyrics, the earlier title being "Smile and Show Your Dimples."

The other Berlin exhibited remarkably subtle taste in occasionally creating songs that are extraordinary in their harmony and modulations. Since Berlin was not skilled at writing music, he always employed a musical secretary to assist him in getting down on paper what he had created with his famous transposing piano (Now at the Smithsonian).   The secretary was probably even more necessary in the creation of the more musically advanced Berlin songs. (Think of "How Deep is the Ocean?") We must assume that Berlin, conscious of the high quality of songs being produced by Kern, Youmans, Gershwin and Porter, felt that he could match them in that endeavor, and he proved he could.   And, whereas Kern's songs were lacking in the newer rhythms, Berlin's exalted in them.   If George Gershwin could create the tricky "Fascinatin' Rhythm." Berlin could respond a few years later his "Puttin' on the Ritz." Both of these songs would push the limits of syncopated rhythm and trick counting schemes. Morover, Berlin's lyrics are his own.

Berlin may have been inconsistent in his reported statement that a bad song was one that didn't earn money. If he had really thought that, there would not be a surviving group of deeply beautiful songs, often for movies, that were not big money-earners. What he probably meant was that if he tried to create a hit, and it failed, then it was a bad song. Certainly there were other times in his long career when he would create songs for other purposes.

Berlin was not alone in the skill of conceiving original songs, and unable to write them out. (Anthony Newley, later in the century, comes to mind.) Berlin's early background, while rich in performance opportunities and promotion, was not involved in learning Music Theory. A list of the various secretaries he employed would probably prove to be a minor "Who's Who" of music.

If it were true that he could only play piano in one key, it certainly didn't prevent him from finding the remote keys and chords (related to his home chord) to which he would occasionally digress. Undoubtedly there must have been times when the secretary would present possible harmonizations that weren't quite what Berlin wanted, that would lead to trial and error until Berlin was satisfied. Upon reflection, there are some songs in this rarified group that reflect a firm belief in attempting bold new moves in song writing. Some more examples are "Soft Lights and Sweet Music," "The Best Thing for You," and "Soft Lights and Sweet Music." These are not the product of a composer limited to simplistic commercial songs.

BERLIN SONGS
Alexander's Ragtime Band
All Alone
All By Myself
Always
Any Bonds Today?
Anything You Can Do
Be Careful, It's My Heart
Best Thing For You, The
Blue Skies
Change Partners
Cheek To Cheek
Count Your Blessings
Couple of Swells, A
Doin' What Comes Natur'ly
Don't Be Afraid Of Romance
Easter Parade (tune from 1917)
Everybody's Doing It
Girl That I Marry, The
God Bless America
Happy Holliday
Heat Wave
How Deep is the Ocean -- JAZZ FAVORITE
I Love a Piano
I've Got My Love to Keep Me Warm
I've Got the Sun in the Morning
Isn't This a Lovely Day?
It Only Happens When I Dance With You
It's a Lovely Day Today
It's a Lovely Day Tomorrow
Lazy
Let's Face the Music and Dance
Let's have Another Cup of Coffee
Let's Take an Old Fashioned Walk
Love and the Weather
Love, You Didn't Do Right By Me
Mandy

Marie
Maybe It's Because I Love You Too Much
Oh, How I Hate to Get Up in the Morning
Play a Simple Melody
Pretty Girl is Like a Melody, A
Puttin' On the Ritz
Remember
Say It Isn't So
Say It With Music
Shaking the Blues Away
Sisters
Soft Lights and Sweet Music
Song is Ended, The
Steppin' Out With My Baby
There's No Business Like Show Business
They Say It's Wonderful
This is the Army, Mr Jones
Top Hat, White Tie and Tails
We Saw the Sea
What'll I Do?
When I Lost You
White Christmas
You Can't Get a Man With a Gun
You Keep Coming Back Like a Song
You're Just In Love

RICHARD RODGERS (1902 TO 1979)

A phenomenal songwriting career in three acts:
I. Lorenz Hart,
II. Oscar Hammerstein II, and
III. On his own and not giving up.

Rodgers was a song-creating workaholic who resisted ever writing anything outside the context of a show. Could he write good melodies without lyrics to guide him? There are several television series for which he produced background music, each of which reveals that he had the knack of functioning independently of lyrics and show/plot guidance. So we must then conclude that it was merely a preference that prevented him from functioning away from lyrics and shows. In a way it is sad because the world would have enjoyed more of his purely instrumental music. And even more unusual, he refused to attempt mere independent song hits. Apparently the stage musical was his passion, and he would not waste a note on pure music marketing.

Rodger's list of prominent and hit songs is twice as long as the others of the Big Five. The Hart Lyrics (roughly 1923 to 1943) brought out of Rodgers a certain kind of melody and harmonization that permitted easy memorization for use in jazz situations. And it seemed that legions of jazz musicians during the era covered by this book, preferred Rodgers/Hart songs more so than that of other composers. And this kind of Rodgers song was undoubtedly the result of Hart's worldly view that reeked of urban sophistication and flirted with cynicism. Rodgers was intuitively matching the quality of Hart's lyrics. But when Rodgers began his association with Oscar Hammerstein II, it was almost as if he had become another composer; one who appreciated Operetta, open-faced honesty and the less worldly aspects of life. Beginning with the show, Oklahoma, young children and school choirs were all singing this newer, more wholesome Rodgers music. World-weary city-types, sophisticates who had been fans of the former Rodgers, and who had always patronized his Broadway shows, were now left in the lurch. Yet the Hart songs had not gone away, and indeed remained ever present on Radio and recordings.

Rodgers must have known about this chameleon aspect of his talent, and he evidently looked forward to the change. Rodgers had always been aware of Hammerstein's work with his hero, Kern, and probably always yearned for some sort of collaboration. So the physical collapse of Hart in the early

1940s furnished Rodgers his opportunity. Hammerstein, plagued by a string of show failures, was more than willing to link up. Together they would dominate Broadway for over 15 years. During his Hammerstein years, it was as if Rodgers became a forward-propelling Herbert, Romberg and Kern all rolled into one. With Hart he had always produced a number of high quality waltzes ("Lover," "The Most Beautiful Girl in the World," etc.), and now he could really indulge in that tendency. By century's end some commentators were even calling him the "Waltz King" of the 20th Century, a label justifiably earned.

But whether it was with the lyrics of Hart, Hammerstein or later lyricists, Rodgers, amid many songs that were excellent to merely serviceable, would occasionally create a profoundly beautiful melody that would distinguish itself in the nations musical conscience. An example would be "Spring is Here." It stands out in irony against the other songs from the show of its origin. While ordinary workaday Rodgers was profitable and certainly popular, this kind of prestige song was so far above his "merely good," that it must have perplexed Rodgers. He could not control the output of "mega" songs, and probably wished he could. It may well be that he never fully understood his own talent, and looked on in wonderment, as he pressed forward to see where that talent would take him.

For the almost twenty years following the death of Hammerstein, Rodgers searched around for another collaborator. He was his own lyricist for one moderately successful show, and then he linked up successively with three younger lyricists (Stephen Sondheim, Sheldon Harnick and Martin Charnin), but seemingly with no success. While these younger men had a better knowledge of the audiences of the 1960s and 70s, apparently Rodgers would not yield in his set ways. It is an unanswerable question whether any hit show would have resulted if Rodgers had yielded to the wishes of these younger lyricists and production people.

Evidently Rodgers' intention was to work on new shows until the very end of his life, and understandably he hoped for one last Broadway hit. But he was unable to match the stupendous success of his earlier days. Moreover, he was now competing with his earlier successes that were popping up again and again through stage revivals and TV film replays. The songs in his final shows, while still showing the old Rodgers craft, lacked spark. And at the same time the taste of the Broadway show-going public had drifted towards more hard-edged productions. A musical based on I Remember Mama, (near the end of his days) might have been a big hit in 1947, but certainly not in the 1970s. Rodgers' long career was simply winding down, and he was growing too old. But at the same time he was experiencing widespread respect and adulation from those who remembered and respected him. His decline in popularity would have been inevitable, but it was perhaps rushed by the expansion of the popular music industry, and the mass media appeal to newer generations with juvenile taste. But, after all this is said, Rodgers' list of successful and prominent songs remains staggering. It is as if several composers were involved.

RODGERS SONGS
All At Once You Love Her
Bali H'ai
Bewitched
Blue Moon
Blue Room
Climb Every Mountain
Dancing On the Ceiling
Do I Hear a Waltz?
Do I Love You Because You're Beautiful?
Do-Re-Mi
Edelweiss
Everything I've Got Belongs To You
Falling In Love With Love
Fellow Needs a Girl, A
Gentleman is a Dope, The
Getting To Know You
Girl Friend, The
Happy Talk
Have You Met Miss Jones? -- JAZZ FAVORITE
Hello Young lovers

Here In My Arms
I Cain't Say No
I Could Write a Book -- JAZZ FAVORITE
I Didn't Know What Time it Was
I Enjoy Being a Girl
I Have Dreamed
I Married an Angel
I Whistle a Happy Tune
I Wish I Were In Love Again
I'm Gonna Wash That Man Right Out of my Hair
If I Loved You
Isn't It Romantic?   -- JAZZ FAVORITE
It Might As Well Be Spring
It Never Entered My Mind
It's a Grand Night for Singing
It's Easy To Remember
Johnny One-Note
June is Bustin' Out All Over
Lady Is a Tramp, The
Little Girl Blue
Loads of Love
Love, Look Away
Lover
Manhattan
Maria
Mimi
Mister Snow
Most Beautiful Girl in the World, The
Mountain Greenery -- JAZZ FAVORITE
My Favorite Things
My Funny Valentine
My Heart Stood Still
My Romance
No Other Love
Oh, What a Beautiful Morning
Oklahoma
Out Of My Dreams
People Will Say We're In Love
Shall We Dance?
So Far
Some Enchanted Evening
Something Wonderful
Sound of Music, The
Spring Is Here -- JAZZ FAVORITE
Surry With the Fringe On Top, The
Sweetest Sounds, The
Ten Cents a Dance
Ten Minutes Ago
That's For Me
There is Nothing Like a Dame
There's a Small Hotel
This Can't Be Love
This Nearly Was Mine
Thou Swell
Wait Till You See Her
We Kiss in a Shadow
What's the Use of Wonderin'?
Where Or When
Where's That Rainbow?
With a Song in My Heart

Wonderful Guy
You Are Beautiful
You Are Too Beautiful
You Took Advantage of Me
You'll Never Walk Alone
Younger than Springtime

As was indicated earlier, Rodgers worked with lyricist Lorenz Hart for 20 years, then with Oscar Hammerstein for about 15 years. After Hammerstein's death, workaholic Rodgers was his own lyricist for one show, and attempted a few other shows with the above listed lyricists.

GEORGE GERSHWIN (1898 TO 1937)

George Gershwin's songs at first resembled commercial simplicity. The song that ultimately earned him the most money was Swanee, one he created during WW I. Later in the l920s he was attempting commercially viable melody with imaginative harmonizations, occasionally linked with tricky syncopated rhythms that went beyond the ragtime rhythms so prevalent then. Also in the early '20s he started working with his lyricist brother, Ira, and before long they had a hit on Broadway. For almost a decade he had been working for the song publishers, demonstrating their songs at the piano for all the top performers who were constantly looking for new material for their acts. He had also worked as a rehearsal pianist for shows in preparation. This is how he built his reputation as an outstanding pianist. He had been meeting all the biggest show business figures of the day who in turn advised and recommended him. He realized that, if he intended to be a successful song composer in the show and song market of his day, he would be competing with Kern, Berlin, Rodgers and Youmans, as well as a host of lesser creators and performers who, for all he knew, would grow to be big figures in the business. And all along, while his reputation as a pianist was growing, he was driven to compose.

He knew he didn't want his image as pianist to overshadow his acceptance as a composer. Then the Rhapsody in Blue premiere in early 1924 made his career plans at once more successful and complicated: pianist or composer, light songs or symphonic pieces? Many people whose opinions he needed and valued seemed to suggest that he either would, or should move beyond mere songs. Backers of shows in the '20s, while not knowing what to make of him, still backed a succession of shows from which emerged an occasional top tune. His energy and ambition kept him moving. When the Great Depression slowed down the success of any shows, he worked on an opera and then moved to Hollywood. The last 13 years of his short life were somewhat divided between at least four roles: genius celebrity, renowned pianist, composer of concert hall music and opera, and songwriter for shows and movies. His creations for the concert hall and a few Broadway flops had everybody in the 1930s's Show Business wondering about his viability as creator of popular music. When at last, and after he and his brother had moved to Los Angeles for film work, an offer came from RKO Pictures to do the songs for an Astaire/Rogers film, they offered him and his brother only half the money they had given Berlin and Kern for their contributions to that series of films. This is, of course, ironic when we consider the song gems he created in his final days.

Gershwin's constant attempts at musical improvement, and his successful experiments with purely instrumental music are reflected in his songs. His fame brought attention to his songs, and in return the songs most often pleased the lay-listener, while often impressing professional musicians. The quality was quite uneven, a fact can be proven by examining his entire song output. His worst songs reveal a Gershwin not generally known. All of the composers in this book had their less successful, and in some instances, bad songs. An interesting experiment would be to hear the ten or twenty worst songs of each. Gershwin's would prove to be equal in that sense. However, the ten or twenty of his best songs, when compared to his competition, attest to his supreme standing. They are hauntingly memorable, and sometimes deeply moving. Here stands a first class talent. And his songs are probably next to those by Rodgers/Hart in numbers of jazz performances during the mid-20th Century. Moreover, the jazz pianists and arrangers of his day and later, most often had to accept his harmonizations as definitive.

GERSHWIN SONGS

Bess, You Is My Woman
Bidin' My Time
Blah, Blah, Blah
But Not for Me   -- JAZZ FAVORITE
By Strauss
Clap Yo' Hands
Do Do Do
Do It Again
Embraceable You
Fascinating Rhythm
Fidgety Feet
Foggy Day, A
For You, For Me, For Evermore
He Loves and She Loves
I Got Plenty O' Nuttin'
I Got Rhythm
I Loves You, Porgy
I'll Build a Stairway to Paradise
I've Got a Crush On You
It Ain't Necessarily So
Let's Call the Whole Thing Off
Liza
Love Is Here To Stay
Love is Sweeping the Country
Love Walked In
Man I Love, The
Maybe
Mine
Nice Work If You Can Get It
Nobody But You
Of Thee I Sing
Oh Kay
Oh, Lady Be Good -- JAZZ FAVORITE
S'Wonderful
Somebody Loves Me
Someone To Watch Over Me
Soon
Strike Up the Band
Summertime -- JAZZ FAVORITE
Swanee
Sweet and Low-Down
That Certain Feeling
They All Laughed
They Can't Take That Away From Me
Who Cares?

Before Gershwin began an almost exclusive partnership with his lyricist brother, Ira, he had worked with others, such as Irving Caesar, Buddy DeSylva, Oscar Hammerstein II, Otto Harbach and Gus Kahn. There are also song/arias that were created by DuBose Heyward, the librettist of *Porgy and Bess*.

COLE PORTER (1891 to 1964)

He was his own lyricist. It is tempting to talk about the verbal Cole Porter, but since the purpose of this book is more about the music than song texts, that discussion here will be somewhat limited. Porter's appearance on the scene set a new high for sophistication and wide-ranging vocabulary. At the time of his emergence, it is a sure thing that his contemporaneous lyricists scratched their heads in wonderment as they were now hearing words and phrases such as: *ennui*, cocaine, monotone of an evening's drone, pathetic/poetic, Louve Museum, Bendel Bonnet, fol-de-rol, beguine, a memory ever green -- rapture serene, invokes, Tin-Pantithesis, and dilemma. And these words were in highly popular songs! Surely some of the other lyricists must have felt that it was unfair to try competing with such skillful erudition, and maybe they were right. In addition to Porter's learned vocabulary, there were also occasional highly literate phrase constructions, and juxtaposing upper class expressions with that of New York City street talk.   He also pushed the limits of decency with his use of what has been called "café-smut" humor, expressions and attitudes. Broadway people would never hate him for that.

Porter's early career story was ironic in that he struggled to be accepted "from above." Imagine approaching Broadway Producers from a superior economic position. (What would this rich guy know about Broadway shows and songs?) While Porter would never be as rich as the Rockefellers, he certainly had to be the richest individual in the 1920s to ever cajole and convince producers he was the man to do their songs. It is truly an inverted version of the American success story.

Assuming that all of Porter's lyrics are exemplary, it is worth noting that proportionally few (about 50) are the famous songs on which his reputation rests. Yet with those fifty or so songs Porter (arguably) encapsulates the best traits of the songs by Kern, Berlin, Rodgers and Gershwin. When it came to any type of successful song the other four and their lyricists could create, Porter, working all alone, could usually approximate or match them. When it came to melodies and harmonic accompaniments, his Ivy League music education enabled him to create some unforgettable pieces of music that do quite when played as instrumentals.   At the beginning of the 21st Century, America's fascination with Porter's life and his songs seemed to be continually on the rise.

PORTER SONGS
Ace in the Hole
All Of You
All Through the Night
Always True To You In My Fashion
Another Opening, Another Show
Anything Goes
At Long Last Love
Be a Clown
Begin the Beguine
Blow, Gabriel, Blow
Brush Up Your Shakespeare
C'est Magnifique
Ca, C'est L'amour
Do I Love You?
Don't Fence Me In (adapting some else's song)
Easy to Love
Every Time We Say Goodbye
Everything I Love
Friendship
From This Moment On
Get Out of Town
I Concentrate On You
I Get a Kick Out of You
I Love Paris
I Love You -- JAZZ FAVORITE

I've Got My Eyes On You
I've Got You Under My Skin
In the Still of the Night
It's Alright With Me
It's De-Lovely
Just One of Those Things
Let's Be Buddies
Let's Do It
Love For Sale
My Heart Belongs to Daddy
Night and Day
Riding High
Rosalie
So In Love
True Love
Well, Did You Evah?
Were Thine That Special Face
What Is This Thing Called Love?
Why Can't You Behave?
Wunderbar
You Do Something To Me
You'd Be So Nice to Come Home To
You're Sensational
You've Got That Thing
You're the Top

MAJOR LYRICISTS

In spite of the alphabetical listing below, the following were certainly not all equal. Among them are the towering figures: Oscar Hammerstein II, Ira Gershwin, Sammy Cahn, Johnny Mercer, Lorenz Hart, Dorothy Fields, Alan Jay Lerner, and Stephen Sondheim. (I wouldn't even try to rank them.) There is also a possible second list of high dependable professionals, who on occasion helped create high profile songs. These are of special importance: Otto Harbach, Yip Harburg, Howard Dietz, Harold Adamson, the Bergmans, John Burke, Gus Kahn, Mack David, Mack Gordon, Frank Loesser, Mitchell Parish, Ned Washington, and Paul Francis Webster.

Lee Adams, born 1924. Worked primarily with Charles Strouse.

Harold Adamson, 1906-80) Worked with Hoagy Carmichael, Peter DeRose, Walter Donaldson, Vernon Duke, Duke Ellington, Burton Lane, Jimmy McHugh, Vincent Youmans, Victor Young and Sammy Fain.

Marilyn Bergman, born 1929 and Alan Bergman, born 1925. Worked with Sammy Fain, John Mandel, Michel Legrand, Marvin Hamlisch and Henry Mancini.

Henry Blossom, 1866-19. Worked with Victor Herbert.

John Burke, 1908-64. Worked primarily with James Van Heusen.

Irving Caesar, 1895-1996. Worked with George Gershwin and Vincent Youmans.

Sammy Cahn, 1913-93. Worked with Saul Chaplin, Jule Styne and James Van Heusen.

Martin Charnin, born 1934. Worked with Richard Rodgers, Charles Strouse, Vernon Duke, Harold Arlen, and Mary Rodgers.

Hal David, born 1921. Worked with Burt Bacharach

Mack David, 1912-93. Worked with Jerry Livingston, Duke Ellington, John Green, James Van Heusen and Franz Waxman.

Buddy DeSylva, 1895-1950. Worked with George Gershwin, Jerome Kern, Victor Herbert, Nacio Herbert Brown, Richard Whiting and Vincent Youmans.

Howard Dietz, 1896-1983. Main collaborator was Arthur Schwartz.

Dorothy Donnelly, 1880-1928. Worked with Sigmund Romberg.

Al Dubin, 1891-1945. Worked mainly with Harry Warren.

Ray Evans, 1915-2007. Worked with various Hollywood songwriters.

Dorothy Fields, 1905 -74. Worked with Jimmy McHugh, Jerome Kern. Arthur Schwartz, Sigmund Romberg, Harold Arlen, Harry Warren, Burton Lane and Cy Coleman.

Arthur Freed, 1894-73. Worked mainly with Nacio Herbert Brown.

Ira Gershwin, 1896-1982. Though working primarily with his brother George, he also collaborated with Harold Arlen, Vernon Duke, Jerome Kern, Burton Lane, Arthur Schwartz, Vincent Youmans, Harry Warren and Kurt Weill.

Mack Gordon, 1904-1959. Worked with Harry Revel, Harry Warren, Josef Myrow, Ray Henderson, James Van Heusen, Vincent Youmans, and James Monaco.

Oscar Hammerstein II, 1895-1960. Worked first with Sigmund Romberg and Jerome Kern. Then there was the long, successful association with Richard Rodgers.

Otto Harbach, 1873-1963. Worked with Rudolf Friml, Sigmund Romberg, Vincent Youmans, Jerome Kern, and George Gershwin.

E. Y. (Yip) Harburg, 1896-1981. Worked with Harold Arlen and Burton Lane.

Sheldon Harnick, born 1924. Worked mainly with Jerry Bock.

Lorenz Hart, 1895-1943. Worked with Richard Rodgers.

Gus Kahn, 1886-1941. Worked with Walter Donaldson, Isham Jones, Vincent Youmans, George Gershwin, Harry Woods, Victor Schertzinger, Arthur Johnston, Sigmund Romberg and Harry Warren.

Fred Koehler, 1894-1973. Worked primarily with Harold Arlen.

Alan Jay Lerner, 1903-1986). Most famous for his association with Frederick Loewe. he also worked successfully with Burton Lane and Kurt Weill.

Frank Loesser 1910-1969. Before he began writing his own music, he had worked with Burton Lane, Hoagy Carmichael, Jimmy McHugh, Jule Styne, Victor Schertzinger and Arthur Schwartz.

Herbert Magidson 1906-86. Worked with Con Conrad, Sammy Fain, Ben Oakland, Jule Styne, Burton Lane and Jimmy McHugh.

Johnny Mercer 1909-76. Worked with Harold Arlen, Richard Whiting, Hoagy Carmichael, Harry Warren, Gene DePaul, Victor Schertzinger, Henry Mancini, Jerome Kern, Gordon Jenkins, Rube Bloom, Arthur Schwartz and James Van Heusen.

Mitchell Parish 1900-93. Worked with Hoagy Carmichael, Duke Ellington, Peter DeRose and Sammy Fain.

Leo Robin 1900-84, Worked with Vincent Youmans, Richard Whiting, Ralph Ranger, Harry Warren, Jerome Kern, Arthur Schwartz, John Green, Harold Arlen, Jule Styne, Sigmund Romberg and Nacio Herbert Brown.

Billy Rose 1899-1966. Worked with Vincent Youmans, Ray Henderson, Harold Arlen and Harry Warren.

Harry Bache Smith 1860-1936. and
Robert Bache Smith 1875-1951 both worked with Victor Herbert.

Stephen Sondheim, born 1930. Before becoming his own composer, he had worked with Leonard Bernstein, Richard Rodgers and Jule Styne.

Ned Washingon 1901-75. Most famous collaborators were Victor Young, Dimitri Tiomkin and Jimmy McHugh.

Paul Francis Webster 1906-84. Worked with Sammy Fain, Hoagy Carmichael, Duke Ellington, Harry Revel, Rudolf Friml, Jerry Livingston and Dimitri Tiomkin.

P. G. Wodehouse 1881-1975. Worked with Jerome Kern, Sigmund Romberg and Rudolf Friml.

Rida Johnson Young 1869-1926. Worked with Victor Young, Rudolf Friml and Sigmund Romberg.

THE SECOND RANK OF COMPOSERS:

VINCENT YOUMANS (1898 to 1946)

In the 1920s the talent of Vincent Youmans was obvious, for he was the "Toast of Broadway." Though money was never a problem for him, he could easily have retired on the royalties from "Tea for Two." While it is easy to point to formulas found in Youmans' peppy songs, no such formula is possible in explaining his slower melodies. If he hadn't given up on composing, there would have been a "BIG SIX," rather than a "BIG FIVE." Before he began his non-composing final twelve years (1934-46), he exhibited a talent that remained brilliantly alive. The songs "Time On My Hands," "More Than You'll Know," and "Through the Years" reveal a profound emotional depth. Yet, he was to terminate his creative talent at age 35 for enigmatic reasons that will keep everyone guessing. Could it be that this giant of the American popular song was merely angry because operetta producers would not give him a chance to work in that medium? As incongruous as that sounds, it may be close as anyone will ever get to an answer.

Youmans collaborated with a surprising array of lyricists: Ira Gershwin, Herbert Stothart, Otto Harbach, Oscar Hammerstein II, Irving Caesar, Leo Robin, Billy Rose, Edward Eliscu, Edward Heyman, Harold Adamson, Mack Gordon, Buddy DeSylva, and Gus Kahn.

YOUMANS SONGS
Carioca, The
Flying Down to Rio
Great Day
Hallelujah!
I Know That You Know
I Want To Be Happy
Keeping Myself For You
More Than You Know
Music Makes Me
Orchids in the Moonlight
Rise 'n' Shine
Sometimes I'm Happy
Tea for Two
Through the Years
Time On My Hands
Without a Song

Youmans worked with a number of famous lyricists. Among them are Ira Gershwin, Herbert Stothart, Otto Harbach, Oscar Hammerstein II, Irving Caesar, Leo Robin, Billy Rose, Edward Eliscu, Edward Heyman, Harold Adamson, Mack Gordon, Buddy DeSylva, and Gus Kahn.

HAROLD ARLEN (1905 to 1986)

One must conclude that, stylistically, there were two Harold Arlen musical personas, and both were excellent. Early in his career, Harold Arlen was a singer/pianist in nightclubs. This experience would enable him to add a "singer-quality" to songs that professional singers recognize and appreciate to this day. He knew what they needed, and what they liked. And because of his early contacts with shows in the Harlem Cotton Club, he knew how to give songs a special Black Music quality. In fact a number of his songs are a study in Black/Bluesy melodic contours. One could speculate that the archetypical Arlen song is one that shows experience in nightclub performance, and sounds as if a Black created it. Arlen was also the first high-profile popular song composer to occasionally create songs with extra internal measures, thus breaking free of the quadratically perfect 32 measure length. Others had sometimes included extra coda measures, but with Arlen it was true asymmetry.

But there was another side to Arlen. Some of his most successful songs feature mainstream pure melody as practiced by his famous contemporaries, and when hearing them we are surprised to learn the composer is Arlen. (For instance, think of the melodies he created for the film, *The Wizard of Oz*). There might even have been three Arlen personas had any operetta entrepreneurs approached him, for he was raised in a household that was constantly listening to recordings of opera and operetta, and that style of music was supposedly his first love.

ARLEN SONGS
Ac-cen-tchu-ate the Positive
Between the Devil and the Deep Blue Sea
Blues in the Night, The
Come Rain or Come Shine
Evelina
For Every Man There's a Woman
Get Happy
Happiness Is a Thing called "Joe"
Hit the Road to Dreamland
Hooray for Love
I Gotta Right to Sing the Blues
I Love a Parade
I've Got the World On a String
Ill Wind
It's Only a Paper Moon
Last Night When We Were Young
Let's Fall in Love
Lydia, The Tattooed Lady
Man That Got Away, The
My Shining Hour
One for My Baby
Out of this World
Right as the Rain
Sleeping Bee, A
Somewhere Over the Rainbow and the other WIZARD OF OZ songs
Stormy Weather
That Old Black Magic
This Time the Dream's On Me
Today I Love Everybody
When the Sun Comes Out

Arlen's most famous collaborators were Ted Koehler, E. Y. (Yip) Harburg, Johnny Mercer, Ira Gershwin, Lew Brown, Leo Robin, Ralph Blane, Dorothy Fields, Truman Capote, and Dory Previn.

HARRY WARREN (1893 to 1981)

Had Harry Warren held his tongue, not been so self-effacing, and had he not shunned the spotlight, he might have gotten his just due while alive. In a country that appreciates erudition when a public figure speaks, Warren probably always made the wrong impression when he spoke publicly. Here we have an incredibly talented songwriter (Just look at his list!) who, while evidently loving to compose songs, did not care for developing a minimal professional persona, nor an acceptable diplomacy of success. (Many a Show Business figure with as little education as Warren's learned early on to say the right thing at the right time.) One example of his bluntness is famous. It didn't help when he publicly proclaimed that he was using an Oscar statuette (Filmdom's Academy Award) as a doorstop. (In watching a rare TV interview completed very late in his life, the viewer wonders if this rough-toned inarticulate speaker is really the composer many tender songs.) Yet, the dichotomy was there, and we are all the richer because of his talent. Certainly he did not make big money from his songs. Warren's whole career, from 1932 onward, was almost entirely devoted to writing film songs. And since he worked for hire, by law such songs remained (and remain) the property of the studios for which he wrote them. Towards the end of his long life, he claimed that he made more money selling his Beverly Hills house, than from all his songs.

Warren's melodies are a study in balanced and beautiful melodic curvature and satisfying harmonic arching. In spite of the lyrics, it is pure music at its best. He seemed to create mainly from instinct, although one comment in his biography indicates that he could control certain advanced elements. When he submitted "Serenade in Blue," for use in a Glenn Miller film, he said that he knew it was advanced and out of the ordinary because of what it did musically. So, while he knew that his songs were good, he also seemed to know when they were musically challenging.

And, speaking of Glenn Miller, music history was made when Warren crossed paths with him. The songs Warren created for the two Miller films have taken on an almost magical aura, symbolic of the Big Band era. The Miller sound is (arguably) never more historically important than when performing Warren songs. Also, at least two of Warren's songs ("The more I see you" and "There Will Never Be Another You.") were permanently adopted into the repertory of Jazz improvisational ensembles. An even larger group of songs would remain in the common repertory of singers during the Crosby/Sinatra years (circa 1930-70).

WARREN SONGS
About a Quarter To Nine
Acapulco
An Affair to Remember
At Last
Boulevard of Broken Dreams, The
Chattanooga Choo-Choo
Cheerful Little Earful
Forty-Second Street
I Found a Million-Dollar Baby
I Had the Craziest Dream
I Know Why and So Do You
I Love My Baby, My Baby Loves Me
I Only Have Eyes for You
I Wish I Knew
I'll String Along With You
I've Got a Gal in Kalamazoo
If You Feel Like Singing, Sing
It Happened In Sun Valley
Jeepers Creepers
Lady in the Tutti-Fruitti Hat, The
Lullaby of Broadway, The
Lulu's Back in Town
More I See You, The   -- JAZZ FAVORITE
My Heart Tells Me
My One and Only Highland Fling
Nagasaki
On the Atcheson, Topeka and Santa Fe
Remember Me?
September In the Rain
Serenade in Blue
Shadow Waltz, The
She's a Latin from Manhattan
Shipmates Stand Together
Shuffle Off To Buffalo
Song of the Marines
Stanley Steamer, The
That's Amore
There Will Never Be Another You --JAZZ FAVORITE
This Heart of Mine
We're In the Money
Would You Like To Take a Walk?

You Must Have Been a Beautiful Baby
You'll Never Know
You're Getting To Be a Habit With Me
You're My Everything
Zing a Little Zong

Warren's (more famous) Lyricists: Al Dubin, Mack Gordon, Johnny Mercer, Mort Dixon, Billy Rose, Arthur Freed, Leo Robin, and Ralph Blane.

ARTHUR SCHWARTZ (1900 to 1984)

Arthur Schwartz possessed an occasionally deep musical talent. It is occasional because of the large body of songs he produced, many of which are probably just serviceable. Occasionally there would be a haunting, or simply unique melody that would distinguish itself amid all the songs then current. We are lucky that the 1953 MGM film, *The Bandwagon*, was made. Because, in it, are most of the outstanding songs in his catalog. And what songs they are! In all the history of popular song, is there any other song that is quite like "By Myself"? A number of his other songs are just studies in pure melodic beauty. One film song that stands out, and gets virtually no attention is his "Seal It With a Kiss." This song, in operetta style, had a brief life in the 1930s. Its musical phrasing forces itself on to one's musical memory, thus showing how good Schwartz really was, and how wide-ranging was his talent. This song also suggests that somewhere there is a trunk of Schwarz's unsuccessful songs that invites exploration. Who knows what beauty lies there?

SCHWARTZ SONGS
Alone Together
By Myself
Dancing In the Dark
Gal in Calico, A
Haunted Heart
I Guess I'll Have to Change My Plan
I Love Louisa
I See Your Face Before Me
I'll Buy You a Star
If There Is Someone Lovelier Than You
Louisiana Hayride
Magic Moment
New Sun in the Sky
Oh, But I Do
Rainy Night in Rio, A
Shine On Your Shoes, A
Something To Remember You By
That's Entertainment
Then I'll Be Tired Of You
They're Either Too Young, Or Too Old
This is It
Triplets
You and the Night and the Music

Though Schwartz was primarily associated with lyricist Howard Dietz, there were indeed others: Dorothy Fields, Johnny Mercer, Frank Loesser, Oscar Hammerstein II, Edward Heyman, Ira Gershwin, Leo Robin and Al Stillman.

BURTON LANE (1912 to 1997)

If ever there was an underused top-notch talent it was Burton Lane. Anyone who could compose "How About You?" and the songs for *Finian's Rainbow*, and the film *Royal Wedding* had a talent (arguably) the equal of Richard Rodgers'. But apparently a combination of having resided in the Los Angeles area, waiting for film-song commissions, and being too ready to say no to various productions that didn't suit him, resulted in an underused top-notch talent. He tried to make up for it late in his life, but apparently the spark was gone. Opposite examples would be Jule Styne and Arthur Schwartz, both of whom seemed to take everything on. They perhaps knew that even if the production flopped, an outstanding song might still survive. (And that was the case.) But with Lane, the song pickings are slim. We are deprived of many beautiful songs that Lane never wrote. It is unfortunate that Lane's film, *Royal Wedding*, was released in the same year as the attention hogging Gershwin tribute, *An American in Paris*. That, and the Academy rules meant that little attention was paid to the sublime and freshly created group of songs in the Lane film. Luckily, later released CDs have more than proven the point.

LANE SONGS
Come Back to Me
Everything I Have is Yours
Feudin' and Fightin'
How About You?   -- JAZZ FAVORITE
How Are Things in Glocca Morra?
How Could You Believe Me When I...
I Hear Music   -- JAZZ FAVORITE
If This Isn't Love
Lady's In Love With You, The
Look To the Rainbow
Old Devil Moon
On a Clear Day
Something Sort of Grandish
There's a Great Day Coming Manana
Too Late Now
What Did I Have That I Don't Have?
When I'm Not Near the Girl I Love

Lane's most famous lyricists were Harold Adamson, Ralph Freed, Ted Koehler, Al Dubin, E.Y. (Yip) Harburg, Frank Loesser, and Alan Jay Lerner.

JIMMY McHUGH (1894 to 1969)
Jimmy McHugh's songs are competent, serviceable, often unmemorable, and in a very few instances persuasively beautiful. If his style and intent resembles anyone else, it is that of Irving Berlin. There seems to be that same aim of pleasing the common denominator of American society. There were many performances on Radio and TV during the '30s through the 50's, and that brought in many royalty payments. Two of his songs, "I'm in the Mood for Love," and "Don't Blame Me'" both from the mid '30s, would remain jazz favorites of working jazz pianists. In spite of songs in some 21 films and 16 Broadway shows, the highlight of McHugh's career was probably his Frank Sinatra affiliation in a 1943 film. For a brief while, with Sinatra singing some of his best songs ("Where Are You?") on Radio, in films and on recordings, McHugh seemed to be "on top," a position that he never really held. His most unlikely high-profile song was the pleasantly infectious waltz, "It's a Most Unusual Day."

McHUGH SONGS
Can't Get Out of This Mood
Candlelight and Wine
Coming In On a Wing and a Prayer
Cuban Love Song, The
Diga-Diga-Doo
Dinner at Eight
Don't Blame Me -- JAZZ FAVORITE
Exactly Like You
Hinky-Dinky Parlez Vous?
Hubba Hubba Hubba (Dig You Later)
I Can't Believe That You're In Love With Me
I Can't Give You Anything But Love*
I Couldn't Sleep a Wink Last Night
I Feel a Song Coming On

I'm in the Mood for Love -- JAZZ FAVORITE
I'm Shooting High
It's a Most Unusual Day
Lovely Way To Spend an Evening, A
On the Sunny Side of the Street*
South American Way
When My Sugar Walks Down the Street
Where are You?
You're a Sweetheart
  *Bought from Fats Waller?

Of his lyricists, Dorothy Fields, Harold Adamson, Ned Washington, Johnny Mercer and Frank Loesser are the most famous.

DUKE ELLINGTON   (1899 to 1976)

For many, Duke Ellington remains a shining beacon in the world of improvised Jazz, Jazz Composition and in the era of the Big Bands. His originality in popular music has made his recordings and arrangements endure. In this book, we are naturally most interested in his list of surviving songs. And what a list it is!   However, in some instances it is difficult to know just which songs were composed solely by Ellington, and which were the joint effort of the top, and sometimes legendary arrangers and musicians who were in his band. Since Ellington's band was his experimental sounding board, and since he hired the best players, it may be that his players furnished motivic ideas that were then shaped into songs by Ellington. Moreover, when examining printed song sheets of his music, one sees that the authorship is shared by Irving Mills who probably contributed to the lyrics before going to press. So even with those concerns, we will proceed as if Ellington is the sole composer.

In the short, but potent song list given here there is a stylistic consistency of ever enduring jazz and blues elements that make his list stand apart in this book. (An interesting comparison would be with the "Black" flavored songs of Arlen.)   And because Ellington's legacy has increased in value and appreciation over the decades, his songs have taken on an additional "hallowed" status. Certainly that can't be bad for an era that has essentially passed into history.

ELLINGTON SONGS
Caravan*
Do Nothing Till You Hear From Me
Don't Get Around Much Anymore
I Got It Bad, and that Ain't Good
I Let a Song Go Out Of My Heart
I'm Beginning To See the Light
In a Mellow Tone
In a Sentimental Mood
It Don't Mean a Thing If It Ain't Got The Swing
Mood Indigo
Prelude To a Kiss
Satin Doll
Solitude
Sophisticated Lady

*The 1966 Ascap Directory lists a few band members as collaborators.

Ellington's most famous collaborators and lyricists were Billy Strayhorn, Irving Mills, Mitchell Parish, Henry Nemo, Bob Russell, Juan Tizol* and Paul Francis Webster.

Hoagy (Hoagland) Carmichael (1899 to 1981)

While "Stardust" is the pre-eminent prestige song, other than for "The Nearness of You," most of Carmichael's successful songs are of a different character. Rather, he seemed to specialize in cute and catchy songs that 1, had peppy rhythm ("Stardust" was originally intended that way.), 2. had rural atmosphere, 3. suggested a Jazz orientation, and 4. Presented a cracker-barrel philosophy. These were qualities that were appreciated by a broad base of the American public, and it meant high-profile successes for Carmichael. (Think of "Ol' Buttermilk Sky.") Early in his career, after "Stardust" had been slowed down and given romantic lyrics, Carmichael would then forever have the image of the ineffable composer of that famous song. The independent life that song had/has probably loomed large over Carmichael throughout his career. (Could he ever top it, no matter what he created?) He was also versatile enough to occasionally contribute lyrics to the compositions of others.

Moreover, he was a movie personality with membership in the Screen Actors' Guild. Between 1937 and 1952 he appeared with spoken dialogue in some eleven films that were mostly successful. Such films often needed a stereotypical piano-playing advice-giver, and Carmichael was glad to play that role. (That familiar stock character really caught on with Dooley Wilson in the 1942 film *Casablanca*. Hollywood always likes repeating a successful formula. Compare this steriotype with the musician in the book and film of F. Scott Fitzgerald's TENDER IS THE NIGHT, a figure supposedly emulating Vincent Youmans.) Additionally, in the 1950s Carmichael had a pronounced TV presence.

CARMICHAEL SONGS
Can't Get Indiana Off My Mind
Doctor, Lawyer, Indian Chief
Georgia On My Mind (lyrics by Stuart Gorrell, and not Johnny Mercer.)
Heart and Soul
I Get Along Without You Very Well
In the Cool-Cool-Cool of the Evening
Lazy River
Lazybones
Little Old Lady
Memphis in June
Nearness of You, The
Ole Buttermilk Sky
One Morning in May
Rockin' Chair
Skylark -- JAZZ FAVORITE
Small Fry
Stardust   -- JAZZ FAVORITE
Two Sleepy People

Though Carmichael sometimes served as lyricist for other composers (mentioned above), among his own most famous lyricists were Johnny Mercer, Mitchell Parish, Frank Loesser, Stanley Adams, Paul Francis Webster, Harold Adamson and Ned Washington.

THE THIRD RANK (THOUGH USUALLY FIRST RATE SONGS) FINE COMPOSERS CONSIGNED TO LIVING IN THE SHADOW OF THE FIRST TWO RANKS:

Edward C. Babcock
(Pen name: James Van Heusen (1913 to 1990)

James Van Heusen spent very little time facing the song market on his own. He was destined to write film songs for the two top male pop singers, first Bing Crosby, then later Frank Sinatra. His first few hits on his own had attracted the attention of Bing Crosby, and he was brought to Paramount Pictures in Hollywood where he would stay for many years. Van Heusen's high degree of craftsmanship resulted in a string of remarkable songs. Throughout the Crosby/Sinatra phase of his career (1941-circa 1963) he could always count on top interpretations and hit recordings. By 1964 he could have declared his career a success, and not have written another song. However, he continued on to see what else he could accomplish. There were song commissions for various other films, as well as recording studio songs for Frank Sinatra that showed the knack and skill were still there. He also attempted two unsuccessful Broadway shows, the highly entertaining cast recordings of which are still available. Who is to say why Broadway shows fail? Certainly it isn't always the songs. However, upon listening to the CDs of these shows, there seems to be a glaring failing in Van Heusen's talent; one that had never blocked his immense success up to that point. It would seem, as often demonstrated by Cole Porter, that a good show calls for eclectically different styles of songs, and Van Heusen was unprepared , or incapable of that. He had one style of song – his own. It involved romantic love songs, with occasional novelty numbers, and that was that. Maybe a couple of stage numbers could have some peppy rhythms, but that was the limit. One would hesitate to place any blame on his lyricist (Sammy Cahn) who probably supplied lyrics that were too good for Broadway. So the shows failed. In all fairness, the late 60s witnessed an entertainment upheaval that was adversely affecting many careers, and that certainly played a small part. So, though 1967 was an especially hard year for musicals, a good traditional Broadway show would still have had a chance of success. In retrospect, the best way to understand Van Heusen's high position in the Golden Era is to take into account the Crosby/Sinatra songs, the list of which is formidable.

VAN HEUSEN SONGS
All My Tomorrows
All the Way
Aren't You Glad You're You?
But Beautiful
Call Me Irresponsible
Come Blow Your Horn
Come Dance With Me
Come Fly With Me
Darn That Dream
Everybody Has the Right To Be Wrong
Heaven Can Wait
Here's That Rainy Day   -- JAZZ FAVORITE
High Hopes
Home Before Dark
I Thought About You
I'll Only Miss Her When I Think Of Her
Imagination
It Could Happen to You
It's Always You
Life Is So Peculiar
Like Someone In Love   -- JAZZ FAVORITE
Love and Marriage
Moonlight Becomes You
My Heart Goes Crazy
My Kind of Town

Nancy
Personality
Pocketful of Miracles
Polka Dots and Moonbeams
Second Time Around, The
September of My Years, The
Sleigh Ride in July
Somewhere Along the Way (under a pen name)
Star!
Style
Suddenly It's Spring
Sunday, Monday, or Always
Swinging On a Star
Tender Trap, The
Thoroughly Modern Millie
To Love and Be Loved
Walking Happy
Where Love Has Gone
You, My Love

Van Heusen's lyricists were few: Johnny Mercer, Eddie DeLange, and above all, John Burke, and Sammy Cahn.

Jule Styne (1905 to 1994)

Just as Van Heusen seemingly was incapable of eclecticism (different styles), Jule Styne was the arch-electic of his time. He could create songs that sounded from a bygone era, and he could imitate the styles of his contemporaries. He was indeed extremely versatile. Since his death, his fame and position may even grow, as the consistent beauty of his music becomes more evident. His eclecticism came in handy. What kind of song did the movie or Broadway script call for? He could always more than meet the requirement. Was an old fashioned-sounding song called for? ("Let it Snow," "All I need is the Girl.") A typical Big Band era song ("I've Heard That Song Before") An up-to-date? ("I Don't Want To Walk Without You") An advanced challenging song? ("Ride Through the Night") An infectious dance? ("Together Wherever We Go") In the style of one of his successful contemporaries? (I suspect that "I fall in Love Too Easily" was in the style of Van Heusen, and one account has him admitting that "Time After Time" was in the style of Kern.) He could write in different styles, and apparently often did. As to the quality of his songs: An interesting experiment is to listen to the many film musicals he wrote in the 1940s, when he was a tunesmith in the middle of the Hollywood hierarchy. (For instance, Tonight and Every Night) Even if no hit songs emerged from the film, the songs are still musically memorable and attractive.

Beginning in 1947 he "flexed his muscles" on Broadway with a successful hit. (High Button Shoes). More Broadway hits would follow, mixed in with more movies and shows that either failed or succeeded. (Maybe the show Gypsy was his crowning achievement.) Yet, he always seemed to jump at the chance to write songs. Cast recordings of all his shows are always worth the money. In the early 1960s a literary magazine reported a poll of then-alive famous popular song composers. And most of them wished they had composed Styne's "Just in Time." As he aged, and just like Richard Rodgers (and perhaps others), he continued to attempt another hit Broadway show. I think the both of them preferred to be "carried out on a stretcher" with pen and manuscript paper in their hands.

STYNE SONGS
All I Need is the Girl
As Long As There's Music
Bye Bye, Baby   -- JAZZ FAVORITE
Christmas Waltz, The
Comes Once In a Lifetime
Diamonds Are a Girl's Best Friend
Don't Rain on My Parade
Every Street's a Boulevard in Old New York
Everything's Coming Up Roses

Five Minutes More
Funny Girl
How Do You Speak To an Angel?
I Am Woman
I Don't Want to Walk Without You
I Fall In Love Too Easily
I Still Get Jealous
I'll Walk Alone
I've Heard That Song Before
It's Been a Long, Long Time
It's Magic
It's You, Or No One For Me   -- JAZZ FAVORITE
Just in Time   -- JAZZ FAVORITE
Let It Snow, Let It Snow
Let Me Entertain You
Make Someone Happy
My Own Morning
Never-Never-Land
Papa, Won't You Dance With Me?
Party's Over, The
People
Ride Through the Night
Saturday Night Is the Loneliest Night of the Week
Small World
Some People
Sunday
There Goes That Song Again
Things We Did Last Summer, The
Three Coins in the Fountain
Time After Time
Together Wherever We Go
You'll Never Get Away From Me

Styne acknowledged the importance of his lyricists by claiming that he didn't write "songs," but rather "melodies." (That's a gross simplification because his melodies always implied specific and pleasing harmonic plans.) His collaborators were: Frank Loesser, Sammy Cahn, Leo Robin, Betty Comden & Adolph Green, Robert Hilliard, Stephen Sondheim, and Bob Merrill.

FREDERICK LOEWE (1901 – 1988)
This composer's original citizenship (Austria), temperament, taste and loyalty seemed to really lay in operetta.   However, Alan Jay Lerner's impressive, pertinent lyrics would always prevent that comparison. And if Loewe's heart were really in operetta, it was all the better for us because of his sense of graceful melody and "sensible" harmonization.

LOEWE SONGS
Almost Like Being in Love   -- JAZZ FAVORITE
Camelot
Get Me to the Church On Time
Gigi
Heather On the Hill, The
I Could Have Danced All Night
I Remember It Well
I Talk to the Trees
I'm Glad I'm Not Young anymore
I've Grown Accustomed to Her Face
If Ever I Would Leave You
Night They Invented Champagne, The
On the Street Where You Live
Rain in Spain, The

Thank Heaven for Little Girls
They Call the Wind Maria
With a Little Bit of Luck
Wond'rin' Star
Wouldn't It Be Loverly

FRANK LOESSER (1910 – 1969)

This versatile lyricist/composer first proved himself as a lyricist, aligning himself with a number of other composers presented in this book. But in the late 1940s the opportunity arose for him to show that he needed no collaborator in the creation of successful Broadway shows. That successful odyssey lasted for the last 20 years of his life.

LOESSER SONGS

Adelaide
Anywhere I Wander
Baby, It's Cold Outside
Big D
Bushel and a Peck, A
Guys and Dolls
I Believe In You
I Wish I Didn't Love You So
I'll Know
I've Never Been In Love Before
If I Were a Bell   -- JAZZ FAVORITE
Joey – Joey
Luck Be a Lady
My Darling, My Darling
No Two People
On a Slow Boat to China
Once In Love With Amy
Praise the Lord and Pass the Ammunition
Spring Will Be a Little Late This Year
Standin' On the Corner
Where Are You, Now That I Need You?
Wonderful Copenhagen

SAMMY FAIN (1902 – 1989)

Fain seems to have achieved something few others have. For so short a list here, he had a few powerhouse hit, or acclaimed songs in each of six decades, beginning with the 1920s. Below certain songs have dates by them to illustrate that point.

FAIN SONGS

April Love 1957
By a Waterfall
Certain Smile, A
Dear Hearts and Gentle People 1947
I Can Dream, Can't I?
I'll Be Seeing You
I'm Late
Let a Smile Be Your Umbrella 1927
Love is a Many Splendored Thing
Secret Love
Someone's Waiting for You 1976
Tender is the Night 1961
That Old Feeling 1937   -- JAZZ FAVORITE
Very Precious Love, A
Wedding Bells Are Breaking Up That Old Gang of Mine
When I Take My Sugar to Tea

World That Never Was, A
You Brought a New Kind of Love to Me

Fain's lyricists were Irving Kahal, Paul Francis Webster, E. Y. (Yip) Harburg, Lew Brown, Robert Hilliard, Sammy Cahn, Harold Adamson, Howard Dietz, Alan and Marilyn Bergman, and Mitchell Parish.

Vernon Duke (Vladimir Dukelsky) (1903 to 1969)

This composer, famously, led a double career using the two above names to simulate two different composers. Dukelsky was the composer of symphonic concert music. This was revealed in his autobiography. However, here we are concerned with only his popular songs. The short list here is of the highest quality. The list is short because, while he created many other songs during his career, they were mostly forgettable. Why would so many of his other songs be so bland? It is not convincing to say he was excellent when he worked with certain lyricists. However, to experience a sample of the other side of Duke's song catalog, you are invited to repeatedly watch and listen to the 1951 Warner Brothers Musical April in Paris, so that you can hear and wonder how the forgettable songs in that film are by the same composer as those listed below.

DUKE SONGS

April in Paris
Autumn in New York
Cabin in the Sky
I Can't Get Started -- JAZZ FAVORITE
I Like the Likes of You
Taking a Chance On Love
What is there to Say?

Dukelsky's more famous lyricists were E. Y. (Yip) Harburg, Ira Gershwin, Ogden Nash, Howard Dietz and John Latouche.

Victor Young (1900 to 1956)

Young was the music director for many Paramount films from the late '30s and on. In addition to competent dramatic underscoring, he was that rare figure in Hollywood who could create national-attention-getting melodies. Some were unique musical statements. Like Loesser, death interrupted a career that was on a roll. In the years before Young's death, it seemed that all the movie studios were gladly enlisting his services.

YOUNG SONGS

Around the World in 80 Days
Blue Star (TV Theme)
Ghost of a Chance With You (I don't stand a)
Golden Earrings
Love Letters
Love Me Tonight
My Foolish Heart
Stella By Starlight   -- JAZZ FAVORITE
Street of Dreams
Sweet Sue – Just You
When I Fall in Love   -- JAZZ FAVORITE
Written on the Wind

Young's more famous lyricists were Ned Washington, Edward Heyman, Ray Evans and Jay Livingston.

John Green (1908 to 1989)

Green was an excellent conductor of pit orchestras, radio shows, and later Hollywood movies. He had masterful people-coordinating abilities, and apparently functioned well as an administrator. Early in his career, he created a few* songs which would keep jazz performers and arrangers permanently grateful. Curiously though, it would not be an exaggeration to say that his song output was minimal during his last fifty years.

GREEN SONGS

Body and Soul*
Coquette*
I Cover the Waterfront*
Out of Nowhere*
Raintree County (The Song of)
You're Mine, You*

Green's lyricists were Edward Heyman, E. Y. (Yip) Harburg, Johnny Mercer, Paul Francis Webster, Billy Rose, and Ira Gershwin.

Kurt Weill (1900 to 1950)

He was an escapee from Hitler's Germany, and lived the last fifteen years of his short life in the United States where he enjoyed a number of Broadway successes. Indeed, all of his songs were for stage productions. Weill created songs with a rare and welcome continental tinge to them. Without being told, many uninformed listeners would barely suspect that the following songs are anything but purely American. Good music is good music.

WEILL SONGS

Here I'll Stay
Lost in the Stars
Mack the Knife (Moritat from the Three-Penny Opera)
My Ship   -- JAZZ FAVORITE
September Song, The
Speak Low

Among Weill's highly literate lyricist/librettists were Maxwell Anderson, Marc Blitzstein, Bertold Brecht, Ira Gershwin, Ogden Nash, Alan Jay Lerner and Langston Hughs.

Hugh Martin (born 1914)

Martin's long career probably peaked in the mid-40s when he was at MGM helping to create songs for Judy Garland.

MARTIN SONGS

An Occasional Man
Boy Next Door, The
Buckle Down, Winsoki
Connecticut
Have Yourself a Merry Little Christmas
Love
Pass That Peace Pipe
Tiny Room
Trolley Song, The
You'd Better Love Me While You May

Martin's chief lyricist, who surely was also involved in creating the music, was the versatile Ralph Blane Hunsecker (pen name: Ralph Blane).

THE 1920s & 30s

Most of these songs were introduced in the 1920s-'30s

Isham Jones (1894-1956)
I'll See You In My Dreams 1924 Gus Kahn
It Had To Be You 1924 Gus Kahn
On the Alamo 1922 Gus Kahn
One I Love Belongs To Somebody Else, The 1924 Gus Kahn
Swinging Down the Lane 1923 Gus Kahn
There Is No Greater Love 1936 Marty Symes -- JAZZ FAVORITE

Ralph Rainger (1901-1942)
Blue Hawaii 1937 Leo Robin
Easy Living 1939 Leo Robin -- JAZZ FAVORITE
Faithful Forever 1939 Leo Robin
Here Is My Heart 1934 Leo Robin
If I Should Lose You 1936 Leo Robin
June In January 1934 Leo Robin
Love In Bloom 1934 Leo Robin
My Future Just Passed 1934 Leo Robin
Please 1932 Leo Robin
Sweet is the Word 1937 Leo Robin
Thanks For the Memory (Oscar 1938) Leo Robin
With Every Breath I Take 1934 Leo Robin

Richard Whiting (1891-1938) Was also a lyricist for others
Ain't We Got Fun? 1921 Gus Kahn & Raymond Egan
Beyond The Blue Horizon   with W, Franke Harling 1930 Leo Robin
Breezin' Along with the Breeze   with Haven Gillespie & Seymour Simons 1926
Guilty   with Gus Kahn and & Harry Akst 1931
Honey   with Haven Gillespie & Seymour Simons 1928
Hooray For Hollywood 1937 Johnny Mercer
Japanese Sandman 1920 Raymond Egan
Louise 1929 Leo Robin
My Ideal 1930 Leo Robin
On the Good Ship Lollipop   with Sidney Clare 1934
One Hour With You 1932 Leo Robin
Sleepy-Time Gal   with Ange Lorenzo 1925 Joseph R. Alden & Raymond Egan
Till We Meet Again 1918 Raymond Egan
Too Marvelous For Words 1937 Johnny Mercer
You're An Old Smoothie   with Buddy DeSylva & Nacio Herb Brown 1932

Walter Donaldson (1893-1947)
After I Say I'm Sorry? (What can Say, Dear) with Abe Lyman 1926
At Sundown 1927
Carolina In the Morning 1922 Gus Kahn
Did I Remember? 1936 Harold Adamson
How Ya Gonna Keep 'em Down On the Farm--
        after They've Seen Paree? 1919 Sam Lewis & Joe Young
Little White Lies 1930
Love Me, Or Leave Me 1928 Gus Kahn
My Baby Just Cares For Me 1930 Gus Kahn -- JAZZ FAVORITE
My Blue Heaven 1927 George Whiting
My Buddy 1922 Gus Kahn
My Mammy 1920 Sam Lewis & Joe Young
Romance 1929 Edgar Leslie
Yes Sir, That's My Baby 1925 Gus Kahn

You 1936 Harold Adamson
You're Driving Me Crazy 1930

Harry Ruby (1895-1975)
Give Me the Simple Life (with Rube Bloom) 1945
I Wanna Be Loved By You   with Herbert Stothart 1928 Bert Kalmar
Kiss To Build a Dream On, A   with Bert Kalmar & O. Hammerstein II   1935
Nevertheless   with Bert Kalmar 1931
So-Long Oo-Long, How Long etc.   with Bert Kalmar 1920
Three Little Words 1930 Bert Kalmar
Who's Sorry Now?   With Bert Kalmar & Ted Snyder 1923

Ray Henderson (1906-1970)
Alabamy Bound 1925 Buddy DeSylva & Bud Green
Animal Crackers In My Soup 1935   Ted Koehler & Irving Caesar
Best Things In Life Are Free, The   with Buddy DeSylva & Lew Brown   1927
Birth Of the Blues, The 1926 Buddy DeSylva & Lew Brown
Black Bottom 1926 Buddy DeSylva & Lew Brown
Button Up Your Overcoat 1928 Buddy DeSylva & Lew Brown
Bye Bye Blackbird 1926 Mort Dixon
Five-Foot-Two, Eyes Of Blue 1925   Sam Lewis & Joe Young
Good News 1927   Buddy DeSylva & Lew Brown
If I Had a Talking Picture of You 1929   Buddy DeSylva & Lew Brown
I'm Sitting On Top Of the World 1925   Sam Lewis & Joe Young
It All Depends On You 1926   Buddy DeSylva & Lew Brown
Just a Memory 1927   Buddy DeSylva & Lew Brown
Just Imagine 1927   Buddy DeSylva & Lew Brown
Life Is Just a Bowl of Cherries 1931   Lew Brown
Lucky Day 1926 Buddy DeSylva & Lew Brown
Lucky In Love 1927   Buddy DeSylva & Lew Brown
Sonny Boy   Al Jolson, Buddy DeSylva and Lew Brown 1929
Sunny Side Up 1929   with Buddy DeSylva & Lew Brown
That Old Gang Of Mine 1923   Billy Rose & Mort Dixon
Thrill Is Gone, The   with Lew Brown 1931
Together 1928   Buddy DeSylva & Lew Brown
Varsity Drag, The 1927 Buddy DeSylva & Lew Brown
You're the Cream In My Coffee 1928   Buddy DeSylva & Lew Brown

Con Conrad (Conrad Dober) 1891-1938
Barney Google 1923   Billy Rose
Continental, The 1934 Herb Magidson
Ma, He's Making Eyes At Me 1921   Sidney Clare
Margie   with J. Russell Robinson 1920 Bennie Davis
Memory Lane   with Larry Spier 1924   Buddy DeSylva
Midnight In Paris   with Herb Magidson 1935

Nacio Herb Brown (1896-1964)
All I Do Is Dream Of You 1934 Arthur Freed, lyricist/MGM film producer
Alone 1935 Arthur Freed
Broadway Melody 1929 Arthur Freed
Broadway Rhythm 1935 Arthur Freed
Good Morning 1939 Arthur Freed
I've Got a Feeling You're Fooling 1929 Arthur Freed
Love is Where You Find It 1948 Earl K. Brent
Make 'em Laugh 1953 Arthur Freed
Pagan Love Song 1929 Arthur Freed
Paradise   with Gordon Clifford 1931
Singing In the Rain 1929 Arthur Freed

Temptation 1933 Arthur Freed
Wedding Of the Painted Doll 1929 Arthur Freed
Would You? 1936 Arthur Freed
You Are My Lucky Star 1935 Arthur Freed
You Stepped Out of a Dream 1940 Gus Kahn --JAZZ FAVORITE
You Were Meant For Me 1929 Arthur Freed
You're An Old Smoothie   with Buddy DeSylva & Richard Whiting 1932

Harry Woods (1896 -1970)
I'll Never Say Never Again 1935
I'm Looking Over a Four-Leaf Clover 1927 Mort Dixon
Paddlin' Madelin' Home 1925
River, Stay 'Way From My Door   1931 Mort Dixon
Side By Side 1927
Try a Little Tenderness   with Jimmy Campbell & Reg Connelly 1932
We Just Couldn't Say Goodbye 1932
When the Moon Comes Over the Mountain 1931 Howard Johnson
When the Red, Red Robin Comes Bob.... 1926

Harry Barris (1905-1962)
I Surrender, Dear 1931 Gordon Clifford
It Must Be True 1930 Gus Arnheim & Gordon Clifford
Mississippi Mud   with James Cavanaugh 1927
Wrap Your Troubles In Dreams 1931 Ted Koehler & Billy Moll

Arthur Johnston (1898-1954)
Cocktails For Two   with Sam Coslow   1934
Down the Old Ox Road 1933 Sam Coslow
Just One More Chance 1931 Sam Coslow
My Old Flame   with Sam Coslow 1934
One, Two, Button Your Shoe 1936   John Burke
Pennies From Heaven 1936 John Burke -- JAZZ FAVORITE
So Do I 1936 John Burke
Thanks a Million 1935 Gus Kahn

Harry Revel (1905-1958)
Did You Ever See a Dream Walking? 1933 Mack Gordon
Goodnight My Love 1936 Mack Gordon
Jet (My Love) 1951 Bennie Benjamin & George David Weiss
Love Thy Neighbor 1934   Mack Gordon
Paris In the Spring 1935   Mack Gordon
Stay As Sweet As You Are 1934   Mack Gordon
With My Eyes Wide Open 1934 Mack Gordon

Ray Noble (1903-1978) British
Goodnight Sweetheart   with Jimmy Campbell, Reg Connely & Rudy Vallee 1931
I Hadn't Anyone Till You 1938
Love Is the Sweetest Thing 1933
Love Locked Out 1933 Max Kester
Touch Of Your Lips, The 1936
Very Thought Of You, The 1934

Fred Ahlert (1892- 1953)
I Don't know Why, I Just Do 1931 Roy Turk
I'll Get By 1928 Roy Turk
I'm Gonna Sit Right Down and Write Myself a Letter 1935 Joe Young
Mean To Me 1929 Roy Turk

Moon Was Yellow, The 1934 Edgar Leslie
Walking My Baby Back Home   with Roy Turk 1930   -- JAZZ FAVORITE
Where the Blue Of the Night Meets the Gold of the Day with Roy Turk & B. Crosby1931

Thomas (Fats) Waller (1904-1943)
Sold one or more songs to Jimmy McHugh
Ain't Misbehavin'   1929 Andy Razaf -- JAZZ FAVORITE
Honeysuckle Rose   with Andy Razaf 1929   -- JAZZ FAVORITE
Squeeze Me   with Clarence Williams 1925

James Monaco (1885-1945)
I Can't Begin To Tell You 1945 Mack Gordon
I've Got a Pocketful Of Dreams   1938   John Burke
Row Row Row 1912 William Jerome
We Musn't Say Goodbye 1943   Al Dubin
You Made Me Love You   1913   Joseph McCarthy

Ann Ronell (1906 – 1993)
Rain On the Roof 1932
Willow Weep For Me 1932

Ernesto Lucuona (1895 – 1963) Cuban
(Only English lyricists indicated.)
Breeze and I, The 1940 Al Stillman
Jungle Drums   1930 Carmen Lombardo & Charles O'Flynn
Say "Si - Si"   1936 Al Stillman
Siboney 1929 Dolly Morse
Two Hearts That Pass In the Night 1941 Forman Brown

OUTSTANDING INDEPENDENT SONGS
ACHIEVEMENTS BY MANY COMPOSERS
1920s & 1930s
BY HALF-DECADE
(What a Treasure!)

1920-24
Avalon by Vincent Rose and Buddy DeSylva (Al Jolson credit)
Hard Hearted Hannah by Milton Ager, Jack Yellen, Bob Bigelow, and Charles Bates
I'm Just Wild About Harry by Eubie Blake and Noble Sissle
Limehouse Blues by Philip Braham and Douglas Furber
Love Nest by Louis A. Hirsch and Otto Harbach
Whispering by Richard Coburn, Vincent Rose and John Schonberger

1925-29
Am I Blue? by Harry Akst & Grant Clarke
Back In Your Own Back Yard Dave Dreyer, Billy Rose and (Al Jolson credit)
Can't We Be Friends? by Kay Swift and Paul James
Deed I Do   Walter Hirsch and Fred Rose -- JAZZ FAVORITE
Diane   Lew Pollack and Erno Rapee
Dinah   Harry Akst and Joe Young
Garden In the Rain, A   by Carroll Gibbons and James Dyrenforth
I May Be Wrong, But I Think You're Wonderful by Henry Sullivan and Harry Ruskin

Just You, Just Me by Jesse Greer and Raymond Klages
If I Had You   Jimmy Campbell, Reg Connelly and Ted Shapero
Moonlight On the Ganges   Sherman Myers and Chester Wallace
Rain   Eugene Ford, Carey Morgan and Arthur Swanstrom
She's Funny That Way   Neil Moret (words by Richard Whiting)
Sposin'   Paul Denniker and Andy Razaf
Sweet Georgia Brown   Ben Bernie, Kenneth Casey and Maceo Pinkard --- JAZZ FAVORITE
Sweet Lorraine   Cliff Burwell and Mitchell Parish

1930-34

Adios by Enric Madriguera, R. C. Del Campo and Eddie Woods
All of Me by Gerald Marks and Seymour Simons   -- JAZZ FAVORITE
As Time Goes By by Herman Hupfeld
Deep Purple by Peter DeRose and Mitchell Parish
Dream a Little Dream of Me by Fabian Andre, William Schwandt and Gus Kahn
Fine and Dandy by Kay Swift and Paul James
For All We Know by J. Fred Coots and Sam M. Lewis
I'm Getting Sentimental Over You by George Bassman and Ned Washington
Just Friends by John Klenner and Sam Lewis J A Z Z   F A V O R I T E
Moonglow by Eddie DeLange, Wil Hudson and Irving Mills
My Silent Love by Dana Suesse and Edward Heyman
Penthouse Serenade (When we're alone) by Will Jason and Val Burton
Stars Fell On Alabama by Frank Perkins and Mitchell Parish
Sweet and Lovely by Gus Arnheim, Jules Lemare and Harry Tobias
What a Difference a Day Made by Maria Grever and Stanley Adams
When Your Lover Has Gone by E. A. Swan -- JAZZ FAVORITE

1935-39

East Of the Sun by Brooks Bowman
Gone With the Wind by Allie Wrubel and Herb Magidson -- JAZZ FAVORITE
Gypsy In My Soul, The   by Clay Boland and Moe Jaffe
I'll Take Romance by Ben Oakland and Oscar Hammerstein II
Moon Over Miami by Joe Burke and Edgar Leslie
Moonlight Serenade by Glenn Miller and Mitchell Parish
Music Goes 'Round and 'Round, The by Edward Farley, Michael Riley and Red Hodgson
My Own True Love by Max Steiner and 1954 lyrics by Mack David
Night Is Young, and You're So Beautiful by Dana Suesse, Irving Kahal, and Billy Rose
Once In a While by Michael Edwards and Bud Green
Red Sails In the Sunset by Hugh Williams and Jimmy Kennedy
So Rare by Jerry Herst and Jack Sharpe
Stairway To the Stars by Matt Malneck, F. Signorelli and Mitchell Parish
Stompin' At the Savoy by Andy Razof, Benny Goodman, Edgar Sampson and Chick Webb
Sunrise Serenade by Frankie Carle and Jack Lawrence
These Foolish Things Remind Me Of You by Jack Strachey, Harry Link and Holt Marvell
What's New? by Bob Haggart and John Burke
You Turned the Tables On Me by Louis Alter and Sidney Mitchell
Zing! Went the Strings Of My Heart by James F. Hanley

THE 1940s & 50s
Most of these songs were introduced in these decades.

Rube Bloom (1902 to 1976)
Day In -- Day Out 1939 Johnny Mercer
Don't Worry 'Bout Me 1939 Ted Koehler
Fools Rush In 1940 Johnny Mercer
Give Me the Simple Life 1945 Harry Ruby
Maybe You'll Be There 1947 Sammy Gallop

Matt Dennis (1914 to 2002)
Angel Eyes 1953 Earl K. Brent
Everything Happens to Me 1941 Tom Adair
Let's Get Away From It All 1941 Tom Adair
Will You Still Be Mine? 1941 Tom Adair

Gene DePaul (1919 to 1988)
Cow Cow Boogie   with Don Raye 1941
I'll Remember April   with Don Raye 1941 --- JAZZ FAVORITE
Jubilation T. Cornpone 1956 Johnny Mercer
Mr. Five-By-Five   with Don Raye 1942
Star Eyes   with Don Raye 1943
Teach Me Tonight 1953 Sammy Cahn
When You're In Love 1954 Johnny Mercer
You Don't Know What Love Is   with Don Raye 1941

Harold Rome (1908 to 1993)
(His own lyricist)
Fanny 1954
My Heart Sings 1945
South America, Take It Away 1946
Wish You Were Here 1952

Gordon Jenkins (1910 to 1980)
Blue Prelude with Joe Bishop 1933
Goodbye 1935
Married I Can Always Get 1956
P. S. I Love You 1934 Johnny Mercer
San Fernando Valley 1943
This is All I Ask 1963

Victor Schertzinger (1890 to 1941)
Arthur Murray Taught Me Dancing In a Hurry   1942   Johnny Mercer
Dream Lover 1929   Clifford Grey
I Remember You 1942 Johnny Mercer -- JAZZ FAVORITE
One Night of Love   1934   Gus Kahn
Sand in My Shoes 1941   Frank Loesser
Tangerine 1942 Johnny Mercer

Johnny Mercer (1909 to 1976)   (words and music)
Dream 1945
I'm an Old Cow Hand 1936
Something's Gotta Give 1955

Josef Myrow (1910 to 1987)
Autumn Nocturne   1941   Kim Gannon
Kokomo, Indiana   1947   Mack Gordon
On the Boardwalk of Atlantic City   1946   Mack Gordon
Somewhere in the Night   1946   Mack Gordon
You Make Me Feel So Young   1946   Mack Gordon

Frederick Hollander (1896 - 1976)
Falling in Love Again, (Can't Help It)   1930   Sammy Lerner
Moonlight and Shadows   1936   Leo Robin
This is the Moment   1948   Leo Robin
You Leave Me Breathless   1938   Ralph Freed

Jerry Livingston (1909 to 1987)
Bibbidy-Bobbidy-Boo   with Mack David & Al Hoffman   1948
It's the Talk of the Town   1933   Marty Symes & Al Neiberg
Mairzy Doats   with Milton Drake and Al Hoffman   1943
This Is It (Bugs Bunny song) early '40s
Under a Blanket of Blue   1933   Marty Symes & Al Neiberg
Wake the Town and Tell the People   1955   Sammy Gallop
Dream is a Wish Your Heart Makes, A 1948 Mack David & Al Hoffman 1948

Jay Livingston [*No relation to the above.]* (1915 to 2001)
Buttons and Bows   1948   Ray Evans
Marshmallow Moon   1951   Ray Evans
Mona Lisa   1950   Ray Evans
Silver Bells   with Ray Evans 1950
Song of Delilah, The   1949   Ray Evans
Tammy   1957   Ray Evans
To Each His Own   1946   Ray Evans
Whatever Will Be, Will Be (Que Sera, Sera) 1955   Ray Evans
Wish Me a Rainbow 1966 Ray Evans

Dimitri Tiomkin (1900 to 1980)
Friendly Persuasion (Thee I love)   1956   Paul Francis Webster
Green Leaves of Summer, The   1960   Paul Francis Webster
High and the Mighty, The   1954   Ned Washington
High Noon (Do Not Forsake Me)   1952 Ned Washington
Search for Paradise 1957   Ned Washington
Strange are the Ways of Love   1959   Ned Washington
Town Without Pity, A   1961   Ned Washington
Wild is the Wind   1957   Ned Washington

Robert Allen (1928 to 2000)
Chances Are   1957 Al Stillman
Home for the Holidays 1954 Al Stillman
It's Not For Me To Say 1957 Al Stillman
Moments to Remember 1955 Al Stillman
No, Not Much   1956   Al Stillman
You Are Never Far Away From Me 1955   Al Stillman

Richard Adler (born 1921)
(sharing composer/lyrics credit with collaborator Jerry Ross)
Everybody Loves a Lover   1958

Hernando's Hideaway   1954
Hey There   1954
Rags to Riches   1953
Shoeless Joe from Hannibal, Mo.   1955
Steam Heat   1954
Two Lost Souls   1955
Whatever Lola Wants   1955
Ya Gotta Have Heart   1955

Steve Allen (1921 to 2000)
(His own lyricist.)
Gravy Waltz, The   with Ray Brown   1963
I Love You Today 1963
Impossible   1956
This Could Be the Start of Something Big   1956
When I'm in Love   1963

Branislaw Kaper (1902 to 1983)
All God's Chillun Got Rhythm   1937 Gus Kahn
Hi-Lilli, Hi-Lo 1952   Helen Deutsch
Invitation 1952
On Green Dolphin Street   1947   Ned Washington   J A Z Z   F A V O R I T E
San Francisco   with Walter Jurmann 1936 Gus Kahn
Somebody Up There Likes Me   1956   Sammy Cahn

Alfred Newman (1901 to 1970)
Adventures in Paradise   1954
Airport Love Theme ("The Winds of Chance")   1970 Paul Francis Webster
Anasasia 1956   Paul Francis Webster
Best of Everything, The 1959   Sammy Cahn
Moon of Manikoora, The 1938   Frank Loesser

Roger Edens (1905 – 1970)
Our Love Affair   1940 Arthur Freed
It's a Great Day for the Irish 1941
Your Words and My Music   1942 Arthur Freed
Pass That Peace Pipe 1947 with Martin and Blane
You're Awful 1949 Comden and Green
On the Town 1949 Comden and Green
You Can Count On Me 1949 Comden and Green
Moses Suposes' 1952 Comden and Green
Born in a Trunk 1954 Leonard Gershe
Bonjour Paris 1957 Leonard Gershe
On How to Be lovely 1957   Leonard Gershe
Think Pink 1957 Leonard Gershe

Nicholas Brodszky (1905 - 1958)
Be My Love 1950 Sammy Cahn
Because You're Mine   1951 Sammy Cahn
I'll Never Stop Loving You   1955 Sammy Cahn
Wonder Why   1950 Sammy Cahn

Bernie Wayne (1920 – 1993)
Blue Velvet with Lee Morris 1951
Laughing On the Outside, Crying On the Inside   1946 Ben Raleigh
There She Is, Miss America 1954
You Walk By 1940   Ben Raleigh

OUTSTANDING INDEPENDENT SONGS
1940s & 1950s
BY HALF-DECADE

This listing is somewhat enlarged by the infusion of songs (riches) from Latin America during the early '40s. And they were always given new English lyrics by Americans. The new WWII generation was coming of age, and it seemed to be totally enraptured with songs, singers, 78 R.P.M. recordings and big bands. Also, it seemed as if WWII increased the need for songs. Immediately after the war a number of French songs were imported. After 1950 there were imports from a number of other European countries.

1940-44
All, or Nothing At All by Arthur Altman and Jack Lawrence
Amapola by Joseph Lacalle and Albert Gamse
Amor by Garbriel Ruiz and Sunny Skylar
Besame Mucho by Chelo Valazquez and Sunny Skylar
Blue Champagne by Grady Watts, Frank Ryerson and Jimmy Eaton   ---JAZZ FAVORITE
Brazil by Ary Barroso and Sidney Russell
Candy by Alex Kramer, John Whitney and Mack David -- JAZZ FAVORITE
Flamingo by Ted Grouya and Edmond Anderson
Frenesi by Alberto Dominguez, Ray Charles and Sidney K. Russell
Green Eyes by Nilo Menendez, Wolfe Gilbert and Eddie Woods
How High the Moon by Morgan Lewis and Nancy Hamilton
I Hear a Rhapsody by George Fragos, Jack Baker and Dick Gasparre
I'll Be Around by Alec Wilder
I'll Never Smile Again by Ruth Lowe
It's a Big Wide Wonderful World by John Rox
It's a Blue World by Robert Wright and Chet Forrest
Lover Man by Jimmy Davis, Ram Ramirez and Jimmy Sherman   --- JAZZ FAVORITE
Maria Elena by Lorenzo Barcelata and Sidney K. Russell
Moonlight in Vermont by Karl Suessdorf and John Blackburn
Oh, Look at Me Now by Joe Bushkin and John DeVries
Perfidia by Alberto Dominguez and Milton Leeds
Poinciana by Nat Simon and Buddy Bernier
Put Your Dreams Away for Another Day by Stephan Weiss, Paul Mann and Ruth Lowe
There, I've Said It Again by Redd Evans and Dave Mann
Tico Tico by Zequinha Abreu and Ervin Drake
When You Wish Upon a Star by Leigh Harline and Ned Washington
Yours by Gonzalo Roig and Jack Sherr

1945-49
Autumn Serenade by Peter DeRose and Sammy Gallop
Baia by Ary Barroso and Ray Gilbert
Beyond the Sea by Charles Trenet and Jack Lawrence
Coffee Song, The by Dick Miles and Robert Hilliard
Come To the Mardi Gras by Max Bulnoes, Milton DeOliviera, Ervin Drake and Jimmy Shirl
Comme Ci, Comme Ca by Bruno Coquatrix, Pierre Dudan, Joan Whitney, Alex Kramer
Day by Day by Paul Weston, Alex Stordahl and Sammy Cahn   --- JAZZ FAVORITE
Early Autumn by Ralph Burns and Johnny Mercer
I Should Care by Paul Weston, Alex Stordahl and Sammy Cahn   --- JAZZ FAVORITE
It's a Good Day by Dave Barbour and Peggy Lee
It's a Pity to Say Goodnight by Billy Reid
Laura by David Raksin and Johnny Mercer   --- JAZZ FAVORITE
Nature Boy by Eden Ahbez
Night Has a Thousand Eyes, The by Jerry Brainin and Buddy Bernier --- JAZZ FAVORITE
Red Roses for a Blue Lady by Roy Brodsky and Sid Tepper
Sentimental Journey by Les Brown, Bud Green and Ben Homer
Symphony by Alex Alstone and Jack Lawrence
Tenderly by Walter Gross and Jack Lawrence

There Are Such Things by Abel Baer, George W. Meyer and Stanley Adams
Vie en Rose, La by Louiguy and Mack David
We'll Be Together Again by Frankie Laine and Carl Fisher
While We're Young by Alec Wilder, Morty Palitz and Bill Engvick

1950-55

Again by Lionel Newman and Dorcas Cochran
Arrivederci Roma by Renato Rascel and Carl Sigman
Because of You by Arthur Hammerstein and Dudley Wilkinson
C'est si Bon by Henri Betti, Andre Hornez and Jerry Seelen
Dansero by Richard Hayman, Sol Parker and Lee Daniels
Don't Ya Go 'Way Mad by Jimmy Mundy, Illinois Jacquet and Al Stillman --- JAZZ FAVORITE
Ebb Tide by Robert Maxwell and Carl Sigman
End of a Love Affair, The by Edward C. Redding
I Left My Heart in San Francisco by George Cory and Douglass Cross
Lazy Afternoon by Jerome Moross and John LaTouche
Lullaby of Birdland by George Shearing and George Weiss
Mademoiselle de Paree by Paul Durand, Mitchell Parish
My One and Only Love by Anton Rubenstein, Guy Wood and Robert Mellin
Petite Waltz by Joe Heyne, E. A. Ellington and Phyllis Claire
Ruby by Heinz Roemheld and Mitchell Parish
Serenata by Leroy Anderson and Mitchell Parish
That's All by Robert Haymes and Alan Brandt
Under Paris Skies by and Hubert Hiraud and Kim Gannon
Unforgettable by Irving Gordon
Young and Foolish by Albert Hague and Arnold Horwitt
Young at Heart by John Richards and Carolyn Leigh

In the late 1950s there were increasing signs that the "Golden Era" style was coming to a close, but it would be a gradual process. A new young generation, raised on Television, increasingly preferred glittering performer/personalities, and a type of music that was louder, had a pronounced basic beat with heavy off-beats, very basic guitar chords (triads), and "gutsy" lyrics that often portrayed juvenile emotions and situations. If songs were romantic, they would not be so in the former manner that used sweet melody and seventh-chord harmony. So, from the perspective of this book, there would be fewer homegrown songs.   At the same time there would be Golden-Era type songs created for films and still more that were imported from other countries. (For example, "Autumn Leaves" originated in France.)

1955-59

Autumn Leaves by and Joseph Kosma and Johnny Mercer   --- JAZZ FAVORITE
Canadian Sunset by Eddie Heywood and Norman Gimbel
Cry Me a River by Arthur Hamilton
Cute by Neal Hefti and Stanley Styne --- JAZZ FAVORITE
How Little We Know by Philip Springer and Carolyn Leigh
I Wish You Love by Charles Trenet and Albert Beach
Longest Walk, The by Eddie Pola and Fred Spielman
Mangoes by Sid Wayne and Dee Libbey
Misty by Erroll Garner and John Burke
My Heart Reminds Me by Camillo Bargoni and Al Stillman
Non Dimenticar by P. G. Redi and Shelley Dobbins
Old Cape Cod by Claire Rothrock, Milton Yakus and Allan Jeffrey
Pete Kelly's Blues by Ray Heindorf and Sammy Cahn
Picnic by George Dunning and Steve Allen
Return to Me by Carmen Lombardo and Danny DiMinno
Summertime in Venice by Icini and Carl Sigman
Unchained Melody by Alex North and Hy Zaret
Young, and Warm and Wonderful by Lou Singer and Hy Zaret

SILVER ERA '60s and '70s
(Experimenters and Traditionalists)

_____

EXPERIMENTERS

(These composers are more daring in their music, and often their songs are tricky to memorize. Also, each is/was capable of creating an occasional old-fashioned song.)

Leonard Bernstein (1918 – 1990)

Whatever the melodic gift is, Bernstein had it. When he was working at the song level, he proved he could devise melodies with harmony that reach into our emotions.

BERNSTEIN SONGS

America
I Feel Pretty
Lonely Town
Lucky To Be Me
New York – New York
Ohio
Some Other Time
Something's Coming
Tonight

Bernstein's lyricists for the above were Betty Comden, Adolf Green, and Stephen Sondheim.

Cy Coleman (1929 - 2004)

Coleman often seemed to push the musical limits of what a popular song could do, and especially in the direction of jazz.

COLEMAN SONGS:

Best is Yet To Come, The
Hey, Big Spender
Hey, Look Me Over
I'm Gonna Laugh You Right Out of My Life
I've Got Your Number
If My Friends Could See Me Now
Pass Me By
Playboy Theme, The
Riviera, The
There's Gotta Be Something Better Than This
Where Am I Going?
Witchcraft

Coleman's lyricists were Carolyn Leigh, Joseph Allen McCarthy, Robert Hilliard, Peggy Lee, Michael Stewart, Betty Comden, Adolph Green, and especially Dorothy Fields,

Michel Legrand (born 1932)

A citizen of France, Legrand's songs exude that seemingly ever-present French trait of constant (and attractive) melodic sequences. (Repeating ideas at other pitch levels.) His American work made a major impact, and opened up interest in his other songs in his native French language. One song (*) may set some sort of record for the sheer number of words/syllables per minute, and may always require a teleprompter for performance.

LEGRAND SONGS:
Hands of Time, The
I Will Wait for You
Once Upon a Summer Time
Pieces of Dreams
Summer Knows, The
Summer Me, Winter Me
Sweet Gingerbread
Watch What Happens
What Are You Doing the Rest of Your Life?
Windmills of Your Mind, The *

Legrand's Hollywood lyricists were Alan and Marilyn Bergman. Some English lyrics of French language songs are by Norman Gimbel.

Marvin Fisher [Don Davis] (1916 - 1993)
Coming from the Fisher near-dynasty of song composers (father, Fred, and sister Doris), Marvin, when linked up with singer Nat King Cole, produced a number of unusually original songs. This would have come about naturally through the arranging experiences he had with big bands in the 1940s. Maybe his entire catalog invites closer scrutiny.

M. FISHER SONGS
Love-wise
Nothing Ever Changes
Something Happens to Me
Strange
When Sunny Gets Blue

Some of his lyricists are not generally known: Jack Segal, Roy Alfred, John Latouche, Bart Howard and Kenward Elmslie.

Antonio Carlos Jobim (1927 - 1994)
These are magnificent imports from Brazil that work well even without their unique bossa nova accompanimental rhythms. Jobim's original approach to songs made a deeply lasting, and seemingly permanent impression on this country's musical awareness. (Bonfa and others likewise added to this treasure, all of which was embraced by the North American Jazz performers.)

JOBIM SONGS
Corcovado (Quiet Nights of Quiet Stars)
Desafinado
Girl from Ipanima, The
How Insensitive
Meditation
Once I Loved
One - Note Samba
Someone to Light Up My Life
Song of the Jet
Triste (Sadness)
Wave

Some of Jobim's lyricists who created English lyrics are Gene Lees, Jon Hendricks, Jessie Cavanaugh and Norman Gimbel,

Burt Bacharach (born 1928)

Perhaps he is the most uniquely commercial composer of his day. His daring melodies, harmony and rhythms clicked with a large segment of the buying public, and on a continuing basis. As is typical of the newer era, swing rhythms were abandoned in favor of simple meters (as opposed to compound meters). Combined with these unique ingredients, many of his songs have a subtle emotional undercurrent, independent of the lyrics. And, building on something Arlen had initiated, there would be an increase of songs that were non-quadratic. Phrases would no longer have to be eight measures long. From the standpoint of Golden Era songs, anyone claiming that such songs would "never sell" need only look at some of Bacharach's successes.

It is the author's opinion that Bacharach reached his summit in the songs he created for the 1972 film LOST HORIZON. Those songs, along with his orchestral arrangements, should be occasionally performed on the symphonic concert stage.

BACHARACH SONGS

Alfie
Arthur's Theme
Blue on Blue
Do You Know the Way to San Jose
House is Not a Home, A
I Say a Little Prayer
I'll Never Fall in Love Again
Living Together
Look of Love, The
Lost Horizon
Magic Moments
Make It Easy On Yourself
One Less Bell to Answer
Promises – Promises
Raindrops Keep Falling On My Head
This Guy's In Love With You
Walk On By
Want to Be Close To You
What the World Needs Now is Love
What's New, Pussycat?
Wives and Lovers
World is a Circle, The

Bacharach's chief lyricist is/was Hal David. Others included Mack David, Paul Anka, Robert Hilliard and Jack Wolf.

Stevie Wonder [Stevland Morris] (born 1950) (his own lyricist)

Of the many songs this composer/lyricist has created, the following seem to have become permanent in the commercial repertory. Certain traditional aspects of their construction make them attractive and timeless without singers.

WONDER SONGS

All is Fair In Love
I Just Called to Say I Love You
My Cherie Amour
You Are the Sunshine of My Life

Stephen Sondheim (born 1930)

Perhaps he is the most original, accomplished and acclaimed lyricist/composer of Broadway shows in the latter part of the 20th Century. Of the many resulting stage songs, the following have assumed a life away from the stage.

SONDHEIM SONGS

Comedy Tonight
Losing My Mind
Broadway Baby
Send In the Clowns

Andre Previn (born 1929)

Among many talents of this important musical figure was the ability to create respectable popular songs for the films he scored, some of which are hauntingly attractive.

PREVIN SONGS

Faraway Part of Town
Goodbye Charlie
Like Blue
Like Young
Second Chance
Valley Of the Dolls (theme)
Why Are We Afraid?
You're Gonna Hear From Me

Previn's lyricist were Dory Langdon Previn, Alan Jay Lerner and Johnny Mercer

`` `` ``

John Lennon (1940 - 1980) and Paul McCartney (born 1942)

(Both share credit for lyrics and music.)

 (There are only three Beatles songs that fit the premise of this book, and they are daring in their musical construction.)
Fool on the Hill, The
Michelle
Yesterday

TRADITIONALISTS

(There's no song like an old-fashioned song. Don't push any boundaries, just create songs that the public can easily recognize. For many the songs would seem anachronistic.)

Charles (Charlie) Chaplin (1889 - 1977)

In creating his historically important films, Chaplin also created some surprisingly commercial melodies to depict certain situations and characters.

CHAPLIN SONGS:

Smile
Eternally
This Is My Song

Chaplin's lyricists are John Turner, Geoffrey Parsons and Chaplin.

Meredith Willson (1902-84)

To American composers, maybe he was the "father" of this point of view, and if not that, then perhaps the earliest and most successful of the traditionalists in the Silver Era. He always created his own lyrics.

WILLSON SONGS

Belly Up to the Bar, Boys
I Ain't Down Yet
It's Beginning to Look a Lot Like Christmas
Lida Rose
May the Good Lord Bless and Keep you
Seventy-Six Trombones
Till There Was You
Trouble (in River City)
You and I (1941)

Henry Mancini (1924 - 1994)

Though at heart an experimenter, the public was more accepting of his old-fashioned songs.

MANCINI SONGS

Charade   (*experimental)
Days of Wine and Roses, The
Dear Heart
I Love You and Don't You Forget It
Latin-Go-Lightly
Loss of Love, The
Mister Lucky TV Theme *
Moon River
Peter Gunn TV Theme, The
Pink Panther Theme, The
Sweetheart Tree, The
Thorn Birds Theme, The
Two for the Road *
Whistling Away the Dark

Among Mancini's more famous lyricists were Johnny Mercer, Leslie Bricusse, Alan and Marilyn Bergman, and Livingston/Evans

Anthony Newley (born 1930)

In some respects Newley resembled Irving Berlin in that he, too, was a professional singer, did his own lyrics and needed a "secretary" to write down his strikingly effective musical melodies. The secretary also probably offered hamonizations for Newley's approval.   Newley is an example of that rare being, the intuitive singing composer who did not play a musical instrument.

NEWLEY SONGS

On a Wonderful Day Like Today
Goldfinger
Joker, The
What Kind of Fool Am I?
Once in a Lifetime
Gonna Build a Mountain
Who Can I Turn To?
Candy Man, The
Feeling Good
Nothing Can Stop Me Now

Marvin Hamlisch (born 1944)

It may be that this gifted composer lost opportunities because of changes in the market place and audience taste. It seems that he has always had more to give than what we've been getting. As of this writing, one hopes more excellent songs are to come.

HAMLISCH SONGS

Last Time I Felt Like This, The
Life is What You Make It
Nobody Does It Better
One
Sunshine, Lollipops and Rainbows
They're Playing My Song
Through the Eyes of Love
Way We Were, The
What I Did For Love

Hamlisch's lyricists were Marilyn and Alan Bergman, Johnny Mercer, Carole Bayer Sager, Edward Kleban, Howard Liebling,

THE USE OF BROADWAY STAGE FORMULAS

Charles Strouse (born 1928)

Here is a first – rate composer. In addition to the Broadway successes listed below, a closer look at all the songs he created for shows that flopped might yield some gems.

STROUSE SONGS

Applause
I Want To Be With You
Kids
Lot of Living to Do, A
Maybe
Night Song (Ravel's Daybreak Scene from *Daphnis*?)
Once Upon a Time
One Boy
Put On a Happy Face
This is the Life
Those Were the Days (Archie Bunker's TV Theme)
Tomorrow

Some of Strouse's lyricists were Sammy Cahn, Lee Adams and Martin Charin.

Jerry Herman (Born 1933)

Especially since he is his own lyricist, Herman is perhaps one of the most successful and favored song creators working within the Theatrical medium.

HERMAN SONGS

Before the Parade Passes By
Hello Dolly
If He Walked Into My Life
It Only Takes a Moment
It's Today
Mame
Put On Your Sunday Clothes
Ribbons Down My Back

So Long, Dearie
We Are What We Are
We Need a Little Christmas

John Kander (born 1930)
Working with his lyricist Fred Ebb, this composer has seemingly had only spotty success. What memorable songs there are have proven most impressive.

KANDER SONGS
Cabaret
Happy Time, The
How Lucky Can You Get?
Married
Maybe This Time
Money – money – money
My Coloring Book
New York – New York – New York
Wilcommen

Harvey Schmidt (born 1929)
He and his lyricist Tom Jones have had a limited list of successful songs.

SCHMIDT SONGS
Honeymoon is Over, The
My Cup Runneth Over With Love
Try to Remember

Jerry Bock (born 1938)
The enormous success of songs in the show FIDDLER ON THE ROOF qualifies this composer for special attention. Credit for the music in his songs was always shared with the particular lyricist with whom he was working.

BOCK SONGS
Mister Wonderful
She Loves Me
Sunrise – Sunset
Till Tomorrow
Too Close For Comfort

Bock's lyricists were Larry Holofcener, George Weiss, Sheldon Harnick

Andrew Lloyd Webber (born 1948)
This acclaimed British stage composer may end up with the distinction of being the most financially successful songwriter of all time. Very few of Webber's stage songs have survived away from the stage. And, even then, these songs seem to cry out for a singer and a stage dramatization.

WEBBER SONGS
Don't Cry For Me, Argentina
I Don't Know How to Love Him
Memory

Webber's lyricists include Tim Rice, Trevor Nunn and poet T. S. Eliot.

THE 1960s & 70s
Most of these songs were introduced in these decades.

1960-64
Al-di-la by Carlo Donida and Erwin Drake
Almost There by Jerry Keller and Gloria Shane
Bluesette by Jean (Toots) Thielemans and Norman Gimble
Can't Help Falling in Love (with you) by Luigi Creatore, H. Perette and George Weiss
Gentle Rain by Luiz Bonfa and Matt Dubey
Good Life, The by Sacha Distel and Jack Reardon
It's a Mad-Mad-Mad-Mad World by Ernest Gold and Mack David
I Wish You Love by Charles Trenet and Lee Wilson
Little Boat (O Barquinho) by Roberto Menescal and Buddy Kaye
Lollipops and Roses by Tony Velona
More by Riz Ortolani, N. Oliviero and Norman Newell
My Kind of Girl by Leslie Bricusse
Nice 'n' Easy by Lew Spence and Marilyn Keith/Bergman and Alan Bergman
Our Day Will Come by Mort Garson and Robert Hilliard
Ricada Bossa Nova by Luiz Antonio and Dialma Ferriera
Stranger on the Shore by Acker Bilk and Robert Mellin
That Sunday (That Summer) by Joe Sherman and George Weiss
Those Were the Days by Gene Raskin (using a folksong)

1965-69
All by D. Colarossi, N. Oliviero, R. Jesse and M. Grudeff
And Roses and Roses by Dorival Caymmi and Ray Gilbert
And We Were Lovers by Elmer Bernstein and Leslie Bricusse
Aquarius by Galt MacDermot, James Rado and Gerome Ragni
Come Saturday Morning by Fred Karlin and Dory Langdon/Previn
Day in the Life of a Fool, A by Luiz Bonfa, Carl Sigman
Daydream by John B. Sebastian
Downtown by Tony Hatch
Eyes of Love, The by Quincy Jones and Bob Russell
Georgy Girl by Tom Springfield and Jim Dale
If I Ruled the World by Cyril Ornadel and Leslie Bricusse
Impossible Dream, The by Joe Darien and Mitchell Leigh
Is That All There Is? by Jerry Leiber and Mike Stoller
Jean by Rod McKuen
Live for Life by Francis Lai and Norman Gimbel
On the South Side of Chicago by Phil Zeller
Sherry by Lawrence Rosenthal and James Lipton
Somewhere My Love (Lara's Theme) by Maurice Jarre and P. F. Webster
Spanish Eyes by Bert Kaempfert, Eddie Snyder and Charles Singleton
Strangers In the Night by Bert Kaempfert, Charles Singleton, Eddie Schneider
Summer Samba by Marcus Valle, Paulo Valle and Norman Gimbel
Time for Us, A by Nino Rota, L. Kusik and E. Schneider
Wonderful Season of Love, The by Franz Waxman and Paul Francis Webster
Wonderful-Wonderful by Sherman Edwards and Ben Raleigh
Yellow Days by A. Careillo and A. Bernstein

1970-74
Ben by Walter Scharf and Donald Black
Day by Day by Stephen Schwartz and John Michael Tabelak
Everything Is Beautiful by Ray Stevens
First Time Ever I Saw Your Face, The by Evan MacColl
For All We Know by Fred Karlin, Robb Wilson and Arthur James

I'd Like To Teach the World To Sing
  by William Backer, Roger Cook, Roquel Davis,and Roger Greenaway
It's Impossible by Canche Manzanero and Sid Wayne
Midnight At the Oasis by David Nichtern
Nadia's Theme by Barry DeVorzon and Perry Botkin Jr.
Never Can Say Goodbye by Clifton Davis
Old Fashioned Way, The by George Garvarevitz and Charles Aznavour
Sing by Joe Raposo
Snowbird by Gene MacLellan
Speak Softly, Love by Rinaldi Rota and Larry Kusik
This Masquerade by Leon Russell
Touch Me In the Morning by Michael Masser and Ron Miller
What Have They Done To My Song, Ma? by Melanie Safka
Where Do I Begin? by Francis Lai and Carl Sigman

1975-79

And the Beat Goes On by Leon Sylvers, Stephen Shockley & William Shelby
Copacabana (At the Copa) by Barry Manilow, Bruce Sussman and Jack Feldman
Deja Vu by Isaac Hayes and Adrienne Anderson
Evergreen by Barbra Streisand and Paul Williams
I Could Be Happy With You by Julie Andrews and Sandy Wilson
I Write the Songs by Bruce Arthur Johnston
I'll Catch the Sun and Never Give It Back Again by Rod McKuen
Just the Way You Are by Billy Joel
Southern Nights by Allen Toussaint
Tie a Yellow Ribbon by Irwin Levine and L. Russell Brown
Top Of the World by John Bettis and Richard Carpenter
Traces by Buddie Buie, Emory Gordy Jr., James B. Cobb Jr.
You Light Up My Life by Joe Brooks

While a number of the above songs from the '70s are indeed distinctive as pieces of music, their approach to melody and harmony, to say nothing of the lyrics, make them seem more typical of the late 20th Century, rather than the dying Golden-Era. Conversely, there are undoubtedly more songs that fit more easily the criteria of this book, but have been unintentionally omitted.

CLOSING COMMENTS

Though the lyrics have been mostly ignored in this book, one cannot help noticing that the lyrics in Golden songs usually dealt with love as a mental state. It was therefore an extremely romantic period. While later eras would have love lyrics in their songs, there were perhaps more pointed references to copulation, rather than to love as an ideal. There would also be songs that addressed society's problems, along attempts to profit from lyrics that dealt with the daily language and most ordinary affairs of the lower rungs of society. It worked. (As one surviving Golden era composer once quipped: "It used to be that you were pleasingly restricted by subject matter and language in lyrics. Now, anything is fair game: the kitchen sink, walking into a room, driving on the highway, etc.) Combine that with guitar basic triads, and there resulted an entirely different approach to music (discussed elsewhere). If the song in an abstract sense has a delicate nature, from the standpoint of the Golden Era, these changes would in turn weigh heavily on the "butterfly's wings." Another difference between the Golden Era, and later developments involves the weight of words versus the music. No matter how engaging the words were in the Golden Era most creators, perhaps unconsciously, were using words to say something musically. After that it seemed song creators were far more interested in using "music" to convey a verbal message. With such an aim, in time it almost doesn't matter what musical effects are used.

The use of the very label "Silver Era" strongly suggests that the Golden one was dying, and a reaction was setting in. This fact is driven home when one scans the Great Song Lists at the end of the book, and looking at the half-decades beginning in 1960. The Golden Era type of song is increasingly out numbered. During the Silver Era a number of songs were created that lovingly emulated the songs from the '20s and '30s. (Sometimes patronizingly so. For instance, how many shows from the 1970s were using supposedly 1920s accompanimental rhythms and patterns that, upon closer examination, weren't used that much in the '20s?) A late 1960s example would be "Sherry" by James Lipton and Lawrence Rosenthal, an attractive song with limited popularity, destined to lose out to the newer harder-edged songs. So, like any Silver Era, there were creators who were advanced, and those who clung to the past (Experimenters and Reactionaries).

By the late 1970s the Golden/Silver Era all but died out, and of course that was disheartening. Even a few of the above listed decade songs in the '70s seem out of place in this book. After 1980 there would be very few songs to come along with melodic/harmonic/rhythmic skill and manner of the earlier age. Such songs were consigned by later chroniclers and music industry hacks to the "show tune" or "easy listening" categories, and they would have limited popularity. One bright spot in the 1960s was the importation of marvelous Bossa Nova songs from Brazil, the excellent construction of which makes them timeless. (see Antonio Carlos Jobim and Luiz Bonfa) And while certain gig and Jazz musicians would continue playing them well into the future, a new era with its different "music" had arrived.

In this newer age there would continue to be many songs, and hits. What I define as the Silver Age involved decades that saw the emergence of Elvis Presley, the Beatles, Joni Mitchell, Bob Dylan, Carol King, John Denver, Roger Miller, Neil Diamond, Paul Simon and Jimmy Webb. They are an overlap. From the '70s and on, America's taste would seemingly be overly occupied with the heavy off-beat Rock rhythm, and eventually various subcategories. Some of them appealed to vast portions of the public. The very word "Rock" for many would come to mean merely popular music. Of the various subcategories of Rock music, there would evolve Disco and Rap music (although its fans would rightly claim a huge difference and a totally different paternity).

There would be several reactions against such loud and (many felt) obvious music. One was Folk Song. An interesting development in the late '60s and early '70s, took place when Folk Song intersected with Popular music. For a brief span there were occasional highly popular songs delivered in the Folk Song manner and style. (Just voice and guitar.) This temporary development will remain for someone else to document.

Another reaction against Rock would be Country Western (CW), a new label on what was formerly rural music from the Southern States. Whatever this kind of music is called, it had been around all during the period covered by this book, but it had not attracted the attention of the country as a whole. But that would change in the last decades of the century, and maybe that was a massive reaction against the harshness of the then seemingly dominant Rock music. Moreover, some CW songs could, and would be interpreted in the Golden Era manner with orchestral arrangements.

But Rock music continued to dominate. The buying public now insisted on a beat so loud that auditory "feeling" supplanted "emotional" feeling. Though the lyrics might change, the actual music might have seemingly endless repetitions. The newer popular music with its "hooks" would become largely existential, to be mostly cast aside after initial profits and consumption. Many of the performers, after a few hits, would likewise seem as if they had been "thrown away."

By the 1990s there would be an increasing obsession on the visual aspects of performances, as if audiences were listening more with their eyes than their ears. Loudness and verbal messages would now pass for inherent musical quality. Many of the public would grow to think that music is the same thing as singers and lyrics. There was now eccentric originality at any price. And there would be a continuation of what had begun in the 1950s: music whose whole purpose, aside from making a profit, was to appeal to the juvenile population. With the sale of sound systems and endless recording releases, people with no real ability in music became "authorities" in music, while those with actual provable music ability were as much as "thrown out of their own house."

(Even wedding reception music for the most part became the sole territory of "disk jockeys," who show up to play their personal stack of once popular recordings. And, incidentally, they follow a practice whereby they increase the already loud volume as the evening progresses. If it has rhythm and is loud, most people seem to conclude that the music is good.)

But as early as the '70s there seemed to be a growing tendency among some to take stock of the past, to look at where we had been, and what had been achieved in those earlier Golden Era years. Maybe the time had come to appreciate the astounding treasury of songs that had accumulated. Incidentally, by century's end all popular music was being marketed and available to the public in various categories. The Golden Age songs, the subject of this book, and as commented above, would be consigned to a category called "Easy Listening."

Bibliography

American Popular Song by Alec Wilder 1972 Oxford Univ. Press

ASCAP BIOGRAPHICAL DICTIONARY, 4TH ed, R. R. Bowker Co. 1980

ASCAP HIT SONGS, 1980s pamphlet

ASCAP --PLAYBACK Magazine biographical articles

BIOGRAPHIES AND AUTOBIOGRAPHIES of various composers and lyricists

BMI pamphlets (various hit lists)

Great Song Thesaurus, The   by Roger Lax & Frederick Smith,
                                                    Oxford Univ. Press 1989

Who Wrote that Song? By Dick Jacobs & Harriet Jacobs,
                                                    Writers' Digest Books 1994

Television specials devoted to individual composers and relevant song periods.

This Was Your Hit Parade by John R. Williams 1973 Courier-Gazette, Inc.

Printed music of the Golden Era

APPENDIX

A GREAT SONG LIST BY HALF – DECADES.   (Popularity)

The following gives a generalized picture of what was popular during the half – decades up to the mid 1970s. Many songs in the earlier part of this book were not as popular as those on this list. Also omitted in this list are those songs that were popular more for their lyrics than for having minimally interesting music. Here there are also some songs listed that go beyond the Golden Age into some later styles not covered in this book. If not indicated otherwise, most are ASCAP songs while BMI songs (post 1940) are usually indicated.

1920-1924

Ain't We Got Fun? ---Raymond B. Egan, Gus Kahn, Richard Whiting
All Alone---Irving Berlin
April Showers---Buddy DeSylva, Louis Silvers
Avalon---Buddy DeSylva, Vincent Rose
Barney Google--Con Conrad, Billy Rose
California, Here I Come---Buddy DeSylva, Joseph Meyer
Carolina In the Morning---Walter Donaldson, Gus Kahn
Charleston---Jimmy Johnson, Cecil Mack
Charlie, My Boy---Ted Fiorito, Gus Kahn
Chicago, That Toddling Town---Fred Fisher
Deep In My Heart, Dear---Dorothy Donnelly, Sigmund Romberg
Do It Again---Buddy DeSylva, George Gershwin
Everybody Loves My Baby---Jack Palmer, Spencer Williams
Fascinating Rhythm---Gershwin brothers
Georgia---Walter Donaldson, Howard Johnson
Golden Days---Dorothy Donnelly, Sigmund Romberg
Hard Hearted Hannah---Milton Ager, Charles Bates, Bob Bigelow, Jack Yellen
How Come You Do Me Like You Do? ---Gene Austin, Roy Begere
I'm Just Wild About Harry---Eubie Blake, Noble Sissle
I'm Nobody's Baby---Benny David, Milton Ager, Lester Santly
I Cried For You---Gus Arnheim, Arthur Freed, Abe Lyman
Indian Love Call---Rudolf Friml, Otto Harbach, Oscar Hammerstein II
It Had To Be You---Isham Jones, Gus Kahn
I Want To Be Happy---Irving Caesar, Vincent Youmans
I'll Be With You In Apple Blossom Time---Neville Fleeson, Albert von Tilzer
I'll Build a Stairway To Paradise---Buddy DeSylva, and the Gershwin brothers
I'll See You In My Dreams---Isham Jones, Gus Kahn
Kiss In the Dark, A ---Buddy DeSylva, Victor Herbert
Limehouse Blues---Philip Braham, Douglas Furber
L'amour-Toujours-L'amour---Rudolf Friml, Catherine Cushing
Lazy---Irving Berlin
Look For the Silver Lining---Jerome Kern, Buddy DeSylva
Love Nest ---Otto Harbach, Louis A. Hirsch
Ma, He's Making Eyes At Me---Sidney Clare, Con Conrad
Man I Love, The ---Gershwin brothers
Margie---Con Conrad, Benny Davis, J. Russell Robinson
My Buddy---Walter Donaldson, Gus Kahn
My Man---Jacques Charles, Channing Pollack, Albert Willemetz, Maurice Yvain
My Time Is Your Time---Leo Dance, Eric Little
Oh, Lady Be Good---Gershwin brothers
One I Love Belongs To Somebody Else, The---Isham Jones, Gus Kahn
Peggy O'Neill---Gilbert Dodge, Ed G. Nelson, Harry Pease
Rose Marie---Rudolf Friml, Otto Harbach, Oscar Hammerstein, Herbert Stothart
Running Wild---A. Harrington Gibbs, Joe Grey, Leo Wood
Say It With Music---Irving Berlin
Second Hand Rose---Grant Clark, James F. Hanley
Serenade---Dorothy Donnelly, Sigmund Romberg
Sheik of Araby---Harry B. Smith, Ted Snyder, Francis Wheeler

Stumbing---Zez Confrey
So Long, oo-long, How Long You Gonna Be Gone?---Bert Kalmer, Harry Ruby
Somebody Loves Me---Buddy DeSylva, George Gershwin, Ballard MacDonald
Song Of Love---Franz Schubert, Sigmund Romberg, Dorothy Donnelly
Swinging Down the Lane---Gus Kahn, Isham Jones
Tea For Two---Irving Caesar, Vincent Youmans
Three O'clock In the Morning---Julian Robledo, Dorothy Terriss
Toot, Toot, Tootsie! (Goo' Bye)---Ernie Erdman, Ted Fiorito, Gus Kahn, Robert A. King
Trees---Joyce Kilmer, Oscar Rasbach
Wabash Blues---Fred Meinken, Dave Ringle
Way Down Yonder In New Orleans---Henry Creamer, J. Turner Layton
What'll I Do?---Irving Berlin
When My Baby Smiles At Me---Ted Lewis, B. Munro, A. B. Sterling, Harry von Tilzer
When My Sugar Walks Down the Street---Gene Austin, Jimmy McHugh, Irving Mills
Whispering---Richard Coburn, John Schonberger, Vincent Rose
Who's Sorry Now?---Bert Kalmer, Harry Ruby, Ted Snyder
Wonderful One---Ferde Grofe, Dorothy Teriss, Paul Whiteman

1925-1929

Ain't Misbehavin'---Harry Brooks, Andy Razaf, Thomas "Fats" Waller
Ain't She Sweet?---Milton Ager, Jack Yellen
Alabamy Bound---Buddy DeSylva, Bud Green, Ray Henderson
Always---Irving Berlin
Am I Blue?---Harry Akst, Grant Clarke
Among My Souvenirs---Edgar Leslie, Horatio Nicholls
At Sundown---Walter Donaldson
Baby Face---Harry Akst, Benny Davis
Back In Your Own Back Yard---Dave Dreyer, Al Jolson, Billy Rose
Best Things In Life Are Free---Lew Brown, Buddy DeSylva, Ray Henderson
Bill---Jerome Kern, Oscar Hammerstein, P.G.Wodehouse
Birth Of the Blues, The ---Lew Brown, Buddy DeSylva, Ray Henderson
Black Bottom---Lew Brown, Buddy DeSylva, Ray Henderson
Blue Room---Lorenz Hart, Richard Rodgers
Blue Skies---Irving Berlin
Breezing Along With the Breeze---Haven Gillespie, Semour Simons, Richard Whiting
Button Up Your Overcoat---Lew Brown, Buddy DeSylva, Ray Henderson
Bye Bye Blackbird---Mort Dixon, Ray Henderson
Can't Help Lovin' Dat Man---Jerome Kern, Oscar Hammerstein II
Can't We Be Friends?---Paul James, Kay Swift
Carolina Moon---Joe Burke, Benny Davis
Cecilia---Dave Dreyer, Herman Ruby
Charmaine---Lew Pollack, Erno Rapee
Chloe---Gus Kahn, Neil Moret
Clap Yo Hands---Gershwin brothers
Collegiate---Moe Jarre, Nat Bonx, Lew Brown
Crazy Rhythm---Irving Caesar, Roger Wolfe Kahn, Joseph Meyer
Deed I Do---Walter Hirsch, Fred Rose
Diane---Lew Pollack, Erno Rapee
Diga Diga Do---Dorothy Fields, Jimmy McHugh
Dinah---Harry Akst, Sam M. Lewis, Joe Young
Do Do Do---Gershwin brothers
Five Foot Two, Eyes Of Blue---Ray Henderson, Sam M. Lewis, Joe Young
Garden In the Rain---James Dyrenforth, Carroll Gibbons
Gimme a Little Kiss, Will Ya, Huh? ---Maceo Pinkard, Jack Smith, Roy Turk
Girl Of My Dreams---Sunny Clapp
Great Day---Edward Elisco, William Rose, Vincent Youmans
Hallelujah---Clifford Grey, Leo Robin, Vincent Youmans
Happy Days Are Here Again---Milton Ager, Jack Yellen
Here In My Arms---Lorenz Hart, Richard Rodgers
Honey---Haven Gillespie, Seymour Simons, Richard Whiting

Honeysuckle Rose---Andy Razaf, Thomas "Fats" Waller
I'm Looking Over a Four-Leaf Clover---Mort Dixon, Harry Woods
I'm Sitting On Top Of the World---Ray Henderson, Sam Lewis, Joe Young
I Can't Believe That You're In Love With Me---Clarence Gaskill, Jimmy McHugh
I Can't Give You Anything But Love---Jimmy McHugh, Dorothy Fields
If I Could Be With You One Hour Tonight---Henry Creamer, Jimmy Johnson
If You Knew Suzie, Like I Know Suzie---Buddy DeSylva, Joseph Meyer
If I Had You---Jimmy Campbell, Reg Connelly, Ted Shapero
I Guess I'll Have To Change My Plan---Howard Dietz, Arthur Schwartz
She's Funny That Way---Neil Moret, Richard Whiting
I Kiss Your Hand, Madame---Fritz Rotter, Sam Lewis, Joe Young, Ralph Erwin
I Know That You Know---Anne Caldwell, Vincent Youmans
I Love My Baby, My Baby Loves Me---Bud Green, Harry Warren
I May Be Wrong But, I Think You're Wonderful---Harry Ruskin, Henry Sullivan
In a Little Spanish Town---Sam M. Lewis, Mabel Wayne, Joe Young
I Never Knew---Ted Fiorito, Gus Kahn
It All Depends On You---Lew Brown, Buddy DeSylva, Ray Henderson
I've Got a Feeling I'm Falling---Harry Link, Billy Rose, Henry Waller
I Found a New Baby---Jack Palmer, Spencer Williams
I Wanna Be Loved By You---Bert Kalmer, Herbert Stothart, Harry Ruby
I Wanna Go Where You Go---Lew Brown, Sidney Clare, Cliff Friend
I'll Get By---Fred Ahlert, Roy Turk
I'll See You Again---Noel Coward
Jealousy---Jacob Gade, Vera Bloom
Jeannine, I Dream Of Lilac Time---L. Wolfe Gilbert, Nathaniel Shilkret
Just You, Just Me---Jesse Greer, Raymond Klages
Keeping Myself For You---Sidney Clare, Vincent Youmans
Let a Smile Be Your Umbrella---Sammy Fain, Irving Kahal, Francis Wheeler
Let's Do It---Cole Porter
Liza---Gershwin brothers and Gus Kahn
Lonesome Road---Gene Austin, Nathaniel Shilkret
Louise---Leo Robin, Richard Whiting
Love Me, Or Leave Me---Walter Donaldson, Gus Kahn
Lover, Come Back To Me---Sigmund Romberg, Oscar Hammerstein
Lucky Day---Lew Brown, Buddy DeSylva, Ray Henderson
Lucky In Love---Lew Brown, Buddy DeSylva, Ray Henderson
Make Believe---Jerome Kern, Oscar Hammerstein II
Making Whoopee! ---Walter Donaldson, Gus Kahn
Manhattan Serenade---Harold Adamson, Louis Alter, Howard Johnson
Marie---Irving Berlin
Me and My Shadow --- Dave Dreyer, Billy Rose
Mean To Me---Fred Ahlert, Roy Turk
Mississippi Mud---Harry Barris, James Cavanaugh
Moonlight and Roses---Ben Black, Edwin H. Lemare, Neil Moret
Moonlight On the Ganges---Sherman Myers, Chester Wallace
More Than You Know---Edward Eliscu, William Rose, Vincent Youmans
Mountain Greenery---Lorenz Hart, Richard Rodgers
My Blue Heaven---Walter Donaldson, George White
My Heart Stood Still---Lorenz Hart, Richard Rodgers
Nagasaki---Mort Dixon, Harry Warren
Ol' Man River---Jerome Kern, Oscar Hammerstein
Pagan Love Song---Nacio Herb Brown
Puttin' On the Ritz---Irving Berlin
Rain---Eugene Ford, Carey Morgan, Arthur Swanstrom
Ramona---L.Wolfe Gilbert, Mabel Wayne
Remember? ---Irving Berlin
Rio Rita---Joseph McCarthy, Harry Tierney
Russian Lullaby---Irving Berlin
St. James Infirmary---Joe Primrose
Should I? ---Nacio Herb Brown, Arthur Freed

Show Me the Way To Go Home---Irving King
Siboney---Ernesto Lecuona, Dolly Morse
Side By Side---Harry Woods
Singing In the Rain---Nacio Herb Brown, Arthur Freed
Sleepy- time Gal---Joseph R. Alden, Raymond B. Egan, Ange Lorenzo, Richard Whiting
Softly As In a Morning Sunrise---Sigmund Romberg, Oscar Hammerstein II
Someone To Watch Over Me---Gershwin brothers
Sometimes I'm Happy---Irving Caesar, Clifford Grey, Vincent Youmans
Song Is Ended, The---Irving Berlin
Sonny Boy---Lew Brown, Buddy DeSylva, Ray Henderson
Soon---Gershwin brothers
Stardust---Hoagy Carmichael, Mitchell Parish
Stout Hearted Men---Sigmund Rombert, Oscar Hammerstein II
Strike Up the Band---Gershwin brothers
Sunny---Jerome Kern, Otto Harbach, Oscar Hammerstein II
Sunny Side Up---Lew Brown, Buddy DeSylva, Ray Henderson
S'posin'---Paul Denniker, Andy Razaf
Sweet and Low Down---Gershwin brothers
Sweet Georgia Brown---Ben Bernie, Kenneth Casey, Maceo Pinkard
Sweet Lorraine---Cliff Burwell, Mitchell Parish
Sweet Sue, Just You---Will J. Harris, Victor Young
S'Wonderful---Gershwin brothers
That Certain Feeling---Gershwin brothers
Then I'll Be Happy---Sidney Clare, Lew Brown, Cliff Friend
Thou Swell---Lorenz Hart, Richard Rodgers
Tip Toe Through the Tulips---Joe Burke, Al Dubin
Valencia---Lucien Boyer, Jacques Charles, Jose Padilla
Varsity Drag--- Lew Brown, Buddy DeSylva, Ray Henderson
Wedding Bells Are Breaking Up That Old Gang Of Mine---Sammy Fain, Irving Cahal, Willie Raskin
What Can I Say After I Say I'm Sorry ---Walter Donaldson, Abe Lyman
What Is This Thing Called Love? ---Cole Porter
When Day Is Done---Buddy DeSylva, Robert Kalscher
When It's Springtime In the Rockies---Robert Sauer, Maryhale Woolsey
When the Red Red Robin Comes Bobbin Along---Harry Woods
Who? ---Jerome Kern, Otto Harbach, Hammerstein II
Why Do I Love You? ---Jerome Kern, Oscar Hammerstein II
Why Was I Born? ---Jerome Kern, Oscar Hammerstein II
With a Song In My Heart---Lorenz Hart, Richard Rodgers
Without a Song---Edward Eliscu, William Rose, Vincent Youmans
Yes Sir, That's My Baby---Walter Donaldson, Gus Kahn
You're the Cream In My Coffee--Lew Brown, Buddy DeSylva, Ray Henderson
You Do Something To Me---Cole Porter
You've Got That Thing---Cole Porter
You Took Advantage Of Me---Lorenz Hart, Richard Rodgers
You Were Meant For Me---Nacio Herb Brown, Arthur Freed
Zigeuner---Noel Coward

1930-1934
Adios---Eddie Woods, Enric Madriguera
All I Do Is Dream Of You---Nacio Herb Brown, Arthur Freed
All Of Me---Gerald Marks, Semour Simons
All Through the Night---Cole Porter
Alone Together---Howard Deitz, Arthur Schwartz
Anything Goes---Cole Porter
April In Paris---Vernon Duke, E.Y. Harburg
As Time Goes By---Herman Hupfeld
Auf Wiedersehn, My Dear---Milton Ager, Al Goodhart, Al Hoffman, Ed Nelson
Autumn In New York---Milton Duke
Betty Co-Ed---J. Paul Fogarty, Rudy Vallee
Between the Devil and the Deep Blue Sea---Harold Arlen, Ted Koehler

Beyond the Blue Horizon ---W. Franke Harling, Leo Robin, Richard Whiting
Bidin' My Time---Gershwin brothers
Blow Gabriel Blow---Cole Porter
Blue Moon---Rodgers and Hart
Blue Prelude---Joe Bishop, Gordon Jenkins
Body and Soul---Frank Eyton, John Green, Edward Heyman, Robert Sour
Boulevard of Broken Dreams---Al Dubin, Harry Warren
But Not For Me---Gershwin brothers
Bye - Bye Blues---Dave Bennett, Chauncey Gray, Fred Hamm, Bert Lown
Carioca, The---Edward Eliscu, Gus Kahn, Vincent Houmans
Cheerful Little Earful---Ira Gershwin, Billy Rose, Harry Warren
Close Your Eyes---Bernice Petkere
Continental, The---Con Conrad, Herb Magidson
Cottage For Sale, A---Larry Conley, Willard Robison
Cuban Love Song, The ---Dorothy Fields, Jimmy McHugh, Herbert Stothart
Dancing In the Dark---Howard Deitz, Arthur Schwartz
Dancing On the Ceiling---Rodgers and Hart
Deep Purple---Mitchell Parish, Peter DeRose
Did You Ever See a Dream Walking? ---Mack Gordon, Harry Revel
Don't Blame Me---Dorothy Fields, Jimmy McHugh
Dream a Little Dream Of Me---F. Andre, Gus Kahn, W. Schwandt
Easter Parade---Irving Berlin
Embraceable You---Gershwin brothers
Everything I Have Is Yours---Harold Adamson, Burton Lane
Exactly Like You---Dorothy Fields, Jimmy McHugh
Falling In Love Again (Can't Help It)---Frederick Hollander, Sammy Lerner
Fine and Dandy---Paul James, Kay Swift
Flying Down To Rio---Edward Eliscu, Gus Kahn, Vincent Youmans
For All We Know---J. Fred Coots, Sam M. Lewis
Forty-Second Street---Al Dubin, Harry Warren
For You---Joe Burke, Al Dubin
Georgia On My Mind---Stuart Gorrell, Hoagy Carmichael
Get Happy---Harold Arlen, Ted Koehler
Goodnight Sweetheart---Ray Noble, Jimmy Campbell, Reg Connelly, Rudy Vallee
Goofus---Gus Kahn, Wayne King, William Harold
Got a Date With An Angel---Clifford Grey, Sonnie Miller, Joseph Turnbridge, Jack Waller
Granada---Dorothy Dodd, Augustin Lara
Guilty---Harry Akst, Gus Kahn, Richard Whiting
Hands Across the Table---Jean Delettre, Mitchell Parish
Have You Ever Been Lonely? ---George Brown, Peter DeRose
Heartaches---Al Hoffman, John Klenner
Heat Wave---Irving Berlin
How Deep Is the Ocean?---Irving Berlin
I Apologize---Al Hoffman, Ed Nelson, Al Goodhart
I Cover the Waterfront---John Green, Edward Heyman
I Don't Know Why, I Just Do---Fred Ahlert, Roy Turk
I Don't Stand a Ghost Of a Chance With You---Bing Crosby, Ned Washington, Victor Young
I Found a Million Dollar Baby---Mort Dixon, Billy Rose, Harry Warren
If There Is Someone Lovelier Than You---Howard Dietz, Arthur Schwartz
I Get a Kick Out Of You---Cole Porter
I Got Rhythm---Gershwin brothers
I Gotta Right To Sing the Blues---Harold Arlen, Ted Koehler
I Like Mountain Music---James Cavanaugh, Frank Weldon
I Like the Likes Of You---Vernon Duke, E.Y. Harburg
I'll Follow My Secret Heart---Noel Coward
I'll Never Be the Same---Gus Kahn, Matty Malneck, Frank Signorelli
I'll String Along With You---Al Dubin, Harry Warren
Ill Wind---Harold Arlen, Ted Koehler
I Love a Parade---Harold Arlen, Ted Koehler
I Love Louisa---Howard Dietz, Arthur Schwartz

I'm Confessing That I Love You---Doc Dougherty, Al Neiburg, Ellis Reynolds
I'm Getting Sentimental Over You---George Bassman, Ned Washington
In a Shanty In Old Shanty Town---Little Jack Little, John Siras, Joe Young
Inka Dinka Doo---Jimmy Durante, Ben Ryan
I Only Have Eyes For You---Al Dubin, Harry Warren
Isle Of Capri---Will Grosz, Jimmy Kennedy
I Still Get a Thrill Thinking Of You---Benny Davis, J. Fred Coots
Isn't It Romantic? ---Rodgers and Hart
I Surrender Dear---Harry Barris, Gordon Clifford
It Don't Mean a Thing If It Ain't Got That Swing---Duke Ellington, Irving Mills
It Happened In Monterey---William Rose, Mabel Wayne
It Isn't Fair---Richard Himber, Sylvester Sprigato, Frank Warshaur
It's Only a Paper Moon---Billy Rose, E. Y. Harburg, Harold Arlen
It's the Talk Of the Town---Jerry Levinson, Neiburg, Marty Symes
I've Got a Crush On You---Gershwin brothers
I've Got the World On a String---Harold Arlen, Ted Koehler
I've Told Every Little Star---Jerome Kern, Oscar Hammerstein II
I Wanna Be Loved---John Green, Edward Heyman, Billy Rose
June In January---Ralph Rainger, Leo Robin
Just a Gigolo---Julius Brammer, Irving Caesar, Leonello Casucci
Just Friends---Sam Lewis, John Klenner
Keeping Myself For You---Sidney Clare, Vincent Youmans
La Cucaracha---Traditional Spanish
Lady Of Spain---Tolchard Evans, Erell Reaves
Lazy Bones---Hoagy Carmichael, Johnny Mercer
Lazy River---Hoagy Carmichael, Sidney Arodin
Let's All Sing Like the Birdies Sing---S. J. Damerell, T. Evans, H. Tilsley, R. Hargreaves
Let's Fall In Love---Harold Arlen, Ted Koehler
Let's Have Another Cup Of Coffee--Irving Berlin
Life Is Just a Bowl Of Cherries---Lew Brown, Ray Henderson
Little Girl---Francis Henry, Madeline Hyde
Little White Lies---Walter Donaldson
Louisiana Hayride---Howard Dietz, Arthur Schwartz
Love For Sale---Cole Porter
Love In Bloom---Ralph Rainger, Leo Robin
Love Is Just Around the Corner---Lewis E. Gensler, Leo Robin
Love Is Sweeping the Country---Gershwin brothers
Love Is the Sweetest Thing---Ray Noble
Love Letters In the Sand---J. Fred Coots, Charles Kenny, Nick Kenny
Lover---Rodgers and Hart
Love Thy Neighbor---Mack Gordon, Harry Revel
Lullaby Of the Leaves---Bernice Petkere, Joe Young
Mad About the Boy---Noel Coward
Maybe It's Because I Love You Too Much---Irving Berlin
Mimi---Rodgers and Hart
Mine---Gershwin brothers
Mood Indigo---Albany Bigard, Duke Ellington, Irving Mills
Moonglow---Eddie DeLange, Will Hudson, Irving Mills
Moon Was Yellow, The ---Fred Ahlert, Edgar Leslie
My Baby Just Cares For Me---Walter Donaldson, Gus Kahn
My Ideal---Newell Chase, Leo Robin, Richard Whiting
My Little Grass Shack In Kealakekua, Hawaii ---B. Cogswell, T. Harrison, J. Noble
My Old Flame---Sam Coslow, Arthur Johnston
My Shawl---Stanley Adams, Xavier Cugat
Nevertheless---Bert Kalmar, Harry Ruby
New Sun In the Sky---Howard Dietz, Arthur Schwartz
Night and Day---Cole Porter
Night Was Made For Love, The---Otto Harbach, Jerome Kern
Object Of My Affection, The---Jimmy Grier, Coy Poe, Pinky Tomlin
Of Thee I Sing---Gershwin brothers

(I'd Love To Spend) One Hour With You---Leo Robin, Richard Whiting
One Night Of Love---Gus Kahn, Victor Schertzinger
On the Good Ship Lollipop---Sidney Clare, Richard Whiting
On the Sunny Side Of the Street---Dorothy Fields, Jimmy McHugh
Orchids In the Moonlight---Edward Eliscu, Gus Kahn, Vincent Youmans
Out Of Nowhere---John Green, Edward Heyman
Paper Doll---Johnny Black
Paradise---Nacio Herb Brown, Gordon Clifford
Peanut Vendor---Marion Sunshine, L. Wolfe Gilbert, Moises Simons
Penthouse Serenade---Will Jason, Val Burton
Please Don't Talk About Me When I'm Gone---Sidney Clare, Sam H. Stept
Prisoner Of Love---Russ Columbo, Clarence Gaskill, Leo Robin
P. S. I Love You---Gordon Jenkins, Johnny Mercer
Rain---Bill Hill, Peter DeRose
Rain On the Roof---Ann Ronell
Rise 'n' Shine---Buddy DeSylva, Vincent Youmans
Rockin' Chair---Hoagy Carmichael
Santa Clause Is Coming To Town---J. Fred Coots, Haven Gillespie
Say It Isn't So---Irving Berlin
Shadow Waltz, The ---Al Dubin, Harry Warren
She Didn't Say Yes---Otto Harbach, Jerome Kern
Shine On Your Shoes, A---Howard Dietz, Arthur Schwartz
Shuffle Off To Buffalo---Al Dubin, Harry Warren
Sing You Sinners---Sam Coslow, W. Franke Harling
Smile, Darn Ya, Smile---Jack Meskill, Charles O'Flynn, Max Rich
Smoke Gets In Your Eyes---Otto Harbach, Jerome Kern
Soft Lights and Sweet Music---Irving Berlin
Solitude---Eddie Delange, Duke Ellington, Irving Mills
Something To Remember You By---Howard Dietz, Arthur Schwartz
Song Is You, The ---Jerome Kern, Oscar Hammerstein II
Sophisticated Lady---Duke Ellington, Irving Mills, Mitchell Parish
Stars Fell On Alabama---Mitchell Parish, Frank Perkins
Stay As Sweet As You Are---Mack Gordon, Harry Revel
Stormy Weather---Harold Arlen, Ted Koehler
Sweet and Lovely---Gus Arnheim, Jules Lemare, Harry Tobias
Temptation---Nacio Herb Brown, Arthur Freed
Ten Cents a Dance---Rodgers and Hart
That's My Desire---Helmy Kresa, Carroll Loveday
Them There Eyes---Maceo Pinkard, Doris Tauber, William Tracey
There Goes My Heart---Benny Davis, Abner Silver
Three Little Words---Bert Kalmar, Harry Ruby
Thrill Is Gone, The ---Lew Brown, Ray Henderson
Through the Years---Edward Heyman, Vincent Youmans
Time On My Hands---Harold Adamson, Mack Gordon, Vincent Youmans
Touch Of Your Hand, The---Otto Harbach, Jerome Kern
Try a Little Tenderness---Jimmy Campbell, Reg Connelly, Harry Woods
Tumbling Tumbleweeds---Bob Nolan
Under a Blanket of Blue---Jerry Levinson, Al Neiburg, Marty Symes
Very Thought of You, The---Ray Noble
Wagon Wheels---Peter DeRose, Billy Hill
Walking My Baby Back Home---Fred Ahlert, Roy Turk
We Just Couldn't Say Goodbye---Harry Woods
We're In the Money---Al Dubin, Harry Warren
What a Difference a Day Made---Stanley Adams, Maria Grever
What Is There To Say?---Vernon Duke, E. Y. Harburg
When I Take My Sugar To Tea---Sammy Fain, Irving Kahal, Pierre Norman
When the Moon Comes Over the Mountain---Howard Johnson, Harry Woods
When Your Lover Has Gone --- E. A. Swan
Where the Blue of the Night Meets the Gold of the Day--Fred Ahlert, B. Crosby, Roy Turk
Who Cares? ---Gershwin brothers

Who's Afraid of the Big Bad Wolf? ---Frank E. Churchill, Ann Ronell
Willow Weep For Me---Ann Ronell
Winter Wonderland---Felix Bernard, Dick Smith
With My Eyes Wide Open, I'm Dreaming---Mack Gordon, Harry Revel
Would You Like To Take a Walk? ---Mort Dixon, Billy Rose, Harry Warren
Wrap Your Troubles In Dreams---Harry Barris, Ted Koehler, Billy Moll
Yesterdays---Otto Harbach, Jerome Kern
You and the Night and the Music---Howard Dietz, Arthur Schwartz
You Are Too Beautiful---Rodgers and Hart
You Brought a New Kind of Love To Me---Sammy Fain, Irving Kahal, Pierre Norman
You Gotta Be a Football Hero---Buddy Fields, Al Lewis, Al Sherman
I'll String Along With You---Al Dubin, Harry Warren
You Oughta Be In Pictures---Edward Heyman, Dana Suesse
You're An Old Smoothie---Nacio Herb Brown, Buddy DeSylva, Richard Whiting
You're Devastating---Otto Harbach, Jerome Kern
You're Driving Me Crazy---Walter Donaldson
You're Getting To Be a Habit With Me---Al Dubin, Harry Warren
You're My Everything---Mort Dixon, Harry Warren, Joe Young
You're the Top---Cole Porter

1935-1939

All the Things You Are---Oscar Hammerstein II, Jerome Kern
Alone---Nacio Herb Brown, Arthur Freed
And the Angels Sing--- (Traditional) Ziggy Elman, Johnny Mercer
At Long Last Love---Cole Porter
A-tisket A-tasket---Van Alexander, Ella Fitzgerald
Begin the Beguine---Cole Porter
Beer Barrel Polka---Lew Brown, Wladimir Timm, Jaromir Vejvoda
Bei mir bist do schoen--- (Traditional) Sammy Cahn, S. Chaplin, J. Jacobs, S. Secunda
Bess, You Is My Woman---Gershwin brothers, DuBose Heyward
Blue Hawaii---Ralph Rainger, Leo Robin
Boo-Hoo---Edward Heyman, John Loeb, Carmen Lombardo
Broadway Rhythm---Nacio Herb Brown, Arthur Freed
By Myself---Howard Dietz, Arthur Schwartz
Caravan---Duke Ellington, Irving Mills, Juan Tizol
Careless---Eddie Howard, Dick Jurgens, Lew Quadling
Change Partners---Irving Berlin
Cheek To Cheek---Irving Berlin
Darling, Je Vous Aime---Anna Sosenko
Day In--Day Out---Rube Bloom, Johnny Mercer
Deep Purple---Peter DeRose, Mitchell Parish
Did I Remember? --- Harold Adamson, Walter Donaldson
Dipsy Doodle, The---Larry Clinton
Do I Love You---Cole Porter
Donkey Serenade, The ---Chet Forrest, Bob Wright, Herbert Stothart
Don't Be That Way---Mitchell Parish, Benny Goodman
Don't Worry 'Bout Me---Rube Bloom, Ted Koehler
East Of the Sun---Brooks Bowman
Easy To Love---Cole Porter
Easy To Remember---Rodgers and Hart
Empty Saddles---Billy Hill
Falling In Love With Love---Rodgers and Hart
Fine Romance, A---Dorothy Fields, Jerome Kern
Flat Foot Floogie---Bud Green, Slim Gaillard, Slam Stewart
Foggy Day, A---Gershwin brothers
God Bless America (from 1918?)---Irving Berlin
Glory Of Love, The---Billy Hill
Gone With the Wind---Herb Magidson, Allie Wrubel
Goodbye---Gordon Jenkins
Goodnight My Love---Mack Gordon, Harry Revel

Goody Goody---Matt Malneck, Johnny Mercer
Gypsy In My Soul, The ---Clay Boland, Moe Jaffe
Harbor Lights, The ---Jimmy Kennedy, Hugh Williams
Heart and Soul---Hoagy Carmichael, Frank Loesser
Heigh-Ho---Frank Churchill, Larry Morey
Hold Tight, Hold Tight --- J. Brandow, L. Kent, E. Robinson, W. Spotswood, L. Ware
I Can Dream, Can't I?---Sammy Fain, Irving Kahal
I Can't Get Started---Vernon Duke, Ira Gershwin
I Concentrate On You---Cole Porter
I Cried For You---Arthur Freed, Gus Arnheim
I Didn't Know What Time It Was---Rodgers and Hart
I Dream Too Much---Dorothy Fields, Jerome Kern
I Feel a Song Coming On---Dorothy Fields, George Oppenheimer, Jimmy McHugh
If I Didn't Care---Jack Lawrence
I Get Along Without You Very Well---Hoagy Carmichael
I Got Plenty Of Nuttin'---Gershwin brothers, Dubose Heyward
I Hadn't Anyone Till You---Ray Noble
I Let a Song Go Out Of My Heart---Duke Ellington, I. Mills, H. Nemo, J. Redmond
I'll Be Seeing You---Sammy Fain, Irving Kahal
I'll Never Say 'Never Again' Again---Harry Woods
I'll Take Romance---Ben Oakland
I'm An Old Cowhand---Johnny Mercer
I Married An Angel---Rodgers and Hart
I'm Gonna Sit Right Down and Write Myself a Letter---Joe Young, Fred Ahlert
I'm In the Mood For Love---Dorothy Fields, Jimmy McHugh
I'm Putting All My Eggs In One Basket---Irving Berlin
I'm Shooting High---Ted Koehler, Jimmy McHugh
Indian Summer---Victor Herbert, Al Dubin
In the Chapel In the Moonlight---Billy Hill
In the Mood---Joe Garland, Andy Razaf
In the Still Of the Night---Cole Porter
Is It True What They Say About Dixie? ---Irving Caesar, Gerald Marks, Sammy Lerner
Isn't This a Lovely Day? ---Irving Berlin
It Ain't Necessarily So---Gershwin brothers
It's De-lovely---Cole Porter
I've Got a Feeling You're Fooling---Nacio Herb Brown, Arthur Freed
I've Got My Eyes On You---Cole Porter
I've Got My Love To Keep Me Warm---Irving Berlin
I've Got You Under My Skin---Cole Porter
I Won't Dance---D. Fields, O. Hammerstein, Otto Harbach, Jerome Kern, Jimmy McHugh
Jeepers Creepers---Johnny Mercer, Harry Warren
Johnny One-Note---Rodgers and Hart
Josephine---Burke Bivens, Gus Kahn, Wayne King
Just One Of Those Things---Cole Porter
Lady In Red, The---Mort Dixon, Allie Wrubel
Lady's In Love With You, The---Burton Lane, Frank Loesser
Lady Is a Tramp, The---Rodgers and Hart
Lamp Is Low, The---Maurice Ravel, Peter DeRose, Mitchell Parish
Let's Call the Whole Thing Off---Gershwin brothers
Let's Face the Music and Dance---Irving Berlin
Little Old Lady---Stanley Adams, Hoagy Carmichael
Love Is Here To Stay---Gershwin brothers
Lovely To Look At---Dorothy Fields, Jerome Kern, Jimmy McHugh
Loved Walked In---Gershwin brothers
Lullaby Of Broadway---Al Dubin, Harry Warren
Lulu's Back In Town---Al Dubin, Harry Warren
Masquerade Is Over, The ---Allie Wrubel, Herb Magidson
Midnight In Paris---Con Conrad, Herb Magidson
Moonlight Serenade---Glenn Miller, Mitchell Parish
Moon Over Miami---Joe Burke, Edgar Leslie

Music Goes 'Round and 'Round, The---Edward Farley, Red Hodgson, Michael Riley
Music, Maestro, Please---Allie Wrubel, Herb Magidson
Muskrat Ramble---Ray Gilbert, Edward Ory
My Funny Valentine---Rodgers and Hart
My Heart Belongs To Daddy---Cole Porter
My Own True Love (Tara's theme)---Mack David, Max Steiner
My Reverie---Claude Debussy, Larry Clinton
My Romance---Rodgers and Hart
Nice Work If You Can Get It---Gershwin brothers
Night Is Young and You're So Beautiful, The---Irving Kahal, Billy Rose, Dana Suesse
Oh, Johnny, Oh!---Ed Rose, Abe Olman
Once In a While---Michael Edwards, Bud Green
Our Love---Peter Tchaikowsky, Buddy Bernier, Larry Clinton, Bob Emmerich
Over the Rainbow---Harold Arlen, E. Y. Harburg
Pennies From Heaven---John Burke, Arthur Johnston
Penny Serenade---Hal Halifax, Melle Weersma
Red Sails In the Sunset---Jimmy Kennedy, Hugh Williams
Rosalie---Cole Porter
September In the Rain---Al Dubin, Harry Warren
September Song---Maxwell Anderson, Kurt Weill
She's a Latin From Manhattan---Al Dubin, Harry Warren
Small Fry---Hoagy Carmichael, Frank Loesser
Solitude---Duke Ellington, Eddie DeLange, Irving Mills
So Rare---Jerry Herst, Jack Sharpe
South Of the Border---Michael Carr, Jimmy Kennedy
Stairway To the Stars---Matt Malneck, Mitchell Parish, Frank Signorelli
Stompin' At the Savoy---Benny Goodman, Andy Razof, Edgar Sampson, Chick Webb
Summertime---George Gershwin, DuBose Heyward
Sunrise Serenade---Frankie Carle, Jack Lawrence
Sweet Leilani---Harry Owens
Thanks a Million---Arthur Johnston, Gus Kahn
Thanks For the Memory---Ralph Rainger, Leo Robin
That Old Feeling---Lew Brown, Sammy Fain
There Is No Greater Love---Isham Jones, Marty Symes
There's a Small Hotel---Rodgers and Hart
These Foolish Things Remind Me of You---Harry Link, Hold Marvell, Jack Strachey
They Can't Take That Away From Me---Gershwin brothers
This Can't Be Love---Rodgers and Hart
Three Little Fishies---Saxie Dowell
Too Marvelous For Words---Johnny Mercer, Richard Whiting
Top Hat, White Tie and Tails---Irving Berlin
Touch of Your Lips, The---Ray Noble
Two Sleepy People---Hoagy Carmichael, Frank Loesser
Undecided---Sid Robin, Charles Shavers
Waltzing Matilda---Marie Cowan, A. B. Paterson
Way You Look Tonight, The---Dorothy Fields, Jerome Kern
We're Off To See the Wizard---Harold Arlen, E. Y. Harburg
What's New? ---Johnny Burke, Bob Haggart
Where Are You? ---Harold Adamson, Jimmy McHugh
Where Or When---Rodgers and Hart
Whistle While You Work---Frank Churchill, Larry Morey
Wishing Will Make It So---Buddy DeSylva
You Are My Lucky Star---Nacio Herb Brown, Arthur Freed
You Go To My Head---J. Fred Coots, Haven Gillespie
You Must Have Been a Beautiful Baby---Johnny Mercer, Harry Warren
You're a Sweetheart---Harold Adamson, Jimmy McHugh
You Turned the Tables On Me---Louis Alter, Sidney Mitchell
Zing! Went the Strings Of My Heart---James F. Hanley

1940-1944   (BMI begins)

Ac-cen-tchu-ate the Positive---Harold Arlen, Johnny Mercer
After You've Gone (from 1918)---Henry Creamer, Turner Layton
Alla En El Rancho Grande (BMI)---Silvano R. Ramos, J. Del Moral
All, or Nothing At All---Arthur Altman, Jack Lawrence
Along the Navajo Trail---
Amapola (BMI)---Albert Gamse, Joseph Lacalle
Amor (BMI)---Sunny Skylar, Ricardo Mendez, Gabriel Ruiz
Angel Eyes---Matt Dennis
Anniversary Waltz---Al Dubin, Dave Franklin
As Time Goes By (from the early 1930s)---Herman Hupfeld
At Last---Mack Gordon, Harry Warren
Autumn Nocturne ---Kim Gannon, Joseph Myrow
Be Careful, It's My Heart---Irving Berlin
Bell Bottom Trousers---Moe Jaffe
Besame Mucho (BMI)---Chelo Velazquez, Sunny Skylar
Bewitched---Rodgers and Hart
Blueberry Hill---Al Lewis, Vincent Rose, Larry Stock
Blues In the Night---Harold Arlen, Johnny Mercer
Boy Next Door, The ---Ralph Blane, Hugh Martin
Brazil (BMI)---Sidney Russell, Ary Barroso
Breeze and I, The (BMI)---Ernesto Lecuona, Al Stillman
Buckle Down, Winsoki---Ralph Blane, Hugh Martin
Candy---Mack David, Alex Kramer, John Whitney
Chattanooga, Choo-Choo---Mack Gordon, Harry Warren
Cherry (BMI)---Don Redman, Ray Gilbert
Close As Pages In a Book---Dorothy Fields, Sigmund Romberg
Coming In On a Wing and a Prayer---Harold Adamson, Jimmy McHugh
Cow - Cow Boogie---Benny Carter, Gene DePaul, Don Raye
Daddy---Bob Troup
Darn That Dream---James Van Heusen, Eddie DeLange
Day Dreaming---Gus Kahn, Jerome Kern
Dearly Beloved---Jerome Kern, Johnny Mercer
Deep In the Heart Of Texas (BMI)---June Hershey, Don Swander
Dolores---Louis Alter, Frank Loesser
Do Nothing Till You Hear From Me---Duke Ellington, Bob Russell
Don't Fence Me In---Cole Porter
Don't Get Around Much Anymore---Duke Ellington, Bob Russell
Don't Sit Under the Apple Tree With Anyone Else But Me-- Lew Brown, Sam Stept, Charles Tobias
Don't Take Your Love From Me---Henry Nemo
Easy Street---Alan Rankin Jones
El Cumbanchero (BMI)---Rafael Hernandez
Elmer's Tune---Elmer Albrecht, Dick Jurgens, Sammy Gallop
Every Time We Say Goodbye---Cole Porter
Flamingo---Ed Anderson, Ted Grouya
Fools Rush In---Rube Bloom, Johnny Mercer
Frenesi (BMI)---Alberto Dominquez, Ray Charles, Sidney K. Russell
Georgia On My Mind (BMI)---Hoagy Carmichael, Stuart Gorrell
Green Eyes (BMI)---Udolfo Utrera, E. Rivera, E. Wood, Nilo Menendez
Hi Neighbor---Jack Owens
How About You?---Ralph Freed, Burton Lane
How High the Moon? ---Nancy Hamilton, Morgan Lewis
Hut Sut Song (BMI)---Les Killion, Ted McMichael
I Cain't Say No---Rodgers and Hammerstein
I Could Write a Book---Rodgers and Hart
I Don't Want To Set the World On Fire (BMI)---E. Durham, B. Benjamin, E. Seiler, S. Marcus
I Don't Want To Walk Without You---Frank Loesser, Jule Styne
I Fall In Love Too Easily---Sammy Cahn, Jule Styne
If It's You---Ben Oakland, Artie Shaw, Milton Drake
I Got It Bad and That Ain't Good---Duke Ellington, Paul Webster

I Had the Craziest Dream---Mack Gordon, Harry Warren
I Hear a Rhapsody (BMI)---George Fragos, Jack Baker, Dick Gasparre
I Hear Music---Burton Lane, Frank Loesser
I'll Be Around (BMI)---Alec Wilder
I'll Never Smile Again---Ruth Lowe
I'll Remember April---Gene DePaul, Pat Johnston, Don Raye
I'll Walk Alone---Sammy Cahn , Jule Styne
I Love You---Cole Porter
Imagination---Johnny Burke, James Van Heusen
I'm Glad There Is You---Paul Madiera, Jimmy Dorsey
I'm Nobody's Baby---Benny Davis, Milton Ager, Lester Suntly
I'm Old-Fashioned---Jerome Kern, Johnny Mercer
In the Blue Of Evening---Tom Adair, Alfred D'Artega
I Remember You---Johnny Mercer, Victor Schertzinger
Is You Is, Or Is You Ain't My Baby? --- Billy Austin, Louis Jordan
It Can't Be Wrong---Max Steiner, Kim Gannon
It Could Happen To You---Johnny Burke, James Van Heusen
It's a Big Wide Wonderful World---John Rox
It's a Blue World---Robert Wright, Chet Forrest
It's a Lovely Day Tomorrow---Irving Berlin
It's Always You---Johnny Burke, James Van Heusen
I've Got a Gal In Kalamazoo---Mack Gordon, Harry Warren
I've Heard That Song Before---Sammy Cahn, Jule Styne
Jersey Bounce, The---Bobby Blater, Tiny Bradshaw, Ed Johnson, Bob Wright
Jim---Caesar Petrillo, Milton Samuels, Nelson Shawn
Jingle-Jangle-Jingle---Joseph Lilley, Frank Loesser
Johnson Rag, The ---Guy Hall, Henry Kleinkauf, Jack Lawrence
Jungle Drums (BMI)---Ernesto Lecuona, Charles Flynn, Carmen Lombardo
Last Time I Saw Paris, The---Jerome Kern, Oscar Hammerstein II
Long Ago and Far Away---Ira Gershwin, Jerome Kern
Lovely Way To Spend An Evening, A---Harold Adamson, Jimmy McHugh
Lover Man---Jimmy Davis, Ram Ramirez, Jimmy Sherman
Magic Is the Moonlight (BMI)---Maria Grever, Charles Pasquale
Mairzy Doats---Milton Drake, Al Hoffman, Jerry Livingston
Malaguena (BMI)---Ernesto Lecuona
Mama Inez (BMI)---Elisio Grenet, L. Wolfe Gilbert
Manhattan Serenade---Harold Adamson, Louis Alter
Maria Elena (BMI)---Sidney K. Russell, Lorenzo Barcelata
Mexicali Rose (BMI)---Jack B. Tenney, Helen Stone
Miss You---Charlie, Harry and Henry Tobias
Moonlight Becomes You---Johnny Burke, James Van Heusen
Moonlight Cocktail---Kim Gannon, Lucky Roberts
Moonlight In Vermont---Karl Suessdorf
More and More---Jerome Kern, E. Y. Harburg
My Devotion---Roc Hillman, Johnny Napton
My Dreams Are Getting Better All the Time---Mann Curtis, Vic Mizzy
My Heart Sings (All of a Sudden) --- Harold Rome, Henri Herpin
My Heart Tells Me---Mack Gordon, Harry Warren   My Own True Love
(Tara's Theme) --- Max Steiner
My Shining Hour---Harold Arlen, Johnny Mercer
My Ship---Kurt Weill, Ira Gershwin
Nearness Of You, The---Hoagy Carmichael, Ned Washington
Nightingale Sang In Berkeley Square, A ---Eric Maschevitz, Manning Sherwin
Oh Look At Me Now---Joe Bushkin
Oh What a Beautiful Morning---Rodgers and Hammerstein
Oklahoma---Rodgers and Hammerstein
One Dozen Roses ---W. Donovan, D. Jurgens, R. Lewis, C. Washburne
One For My Baby---Harold Arlen, Johnny Mercer
Opus (Number) One---Sy Oliver
Paper Doll---Johnny Black

People Will Say We're In Love---Rodgers and Hammerstein
Perdido---Ervin Drake, Hans Lengsfelder, Juan Tizol
Perfidia---Alberto Dominguez, Milton Leeds
Pistol Packin' Mama---Al Dexter
Poinciana---Nat Simon, Buddy Bernier
Praise the Lord and Pass the Ammunition---Frank Loesser
Put Your Dreams Away For Another Day---Stephen Weiss, Paul Mann, Ruth Lowe
Rum and Coca-Cola---Morey Amsterdam, Clotilde Arias, Paul Baron, Jeri Sullivan
San Antonio Rose---Bob Wills
San Fernando Valley---Gordon Jenkins
Saturday Night Is the Loneliest Night Of the Week---Sammy Cahn, Jule Styne
Sentimental Journey---Les Brown, Bud Green, Ben Homer
Serenade In Blue---Mack Gordon, Harry Warren
Shoo-Shoo, Baby---Phil Moore
Skylark---Hoagy Carmichael, Johnny Mercer
Sleepy Lagoon---Jack Lawrence, Eric Coates
Speak Low---Ogden Nash, Kurt Weill
Spring Will Be a Little Late This Year---Frank Loesser
Star Eyes---Gene DePaul, Don Raye
Strange Music---Edvard Grieg, George Forrest, Robert Wright
String Of Pearls, A---Eddie DeLange, Jerry Gray
Sunday, Monday Or Always---Johnny Burke, James Van Heusen
Surrey With the Fringe On Top---Rodgers and Hammerstein
Swinging On a Star---Johnny Burke, James Van Heusen
Taboo---Maria Lecuona, Sidney K. Russell
Take It Easy---Albert DeBru, Vic Mizzy, Irving Taylor
Take the A Train---Billy Strayhorn
Taking a Chance On Love---Vernon Duke, Ted Felter, John LaTouche
Tangerine---Johnny Mercer, Victor Schertzinger
That Old Black Magic---Harold Arlen, Johnny Mercer
There Are Such Things---Stanley Adams, Abel Baer, George Meyer
There Goes That Song Again---Sammy Cahn, Jule Styne
There, I've Said It Again---Redd Evans, Dave Mann
There Will Never Be Another You---Harry Warren
There'll Be Bluebirds Over the White Cliffs Of Dover---Nat Burton, Walter Kent
There'll Be Some Changes Made---W. B. Overstreet, Billy Higgins
There's No You---Adair, Hopper, Durgeon
They're Either Too Young Or Too Old---Frank Loesser, Arthur Schwartz
This Is the Army Mr. Jones---Irving Berlin
This Love of Mine---Sol Parker, Hank Sanicola, Frank Sinatra
Tico Tico---Zequinha Abreu, Ervin Drake
Till Then---Sol Marcus, Eddie Seiler, Guy Wood
Time Waits For No One---Charles Tobias, Cliff Friend
Together---Buddy De Sylva, Lew Brown, Ray Henderson
Tonight We Love---Peter Tchaikowsky, R. Austin, B. Worth, Freddy Martin
Trolley Song, The ---Ralph Blane, Hugh Martin
Tuxedo Junction---Julian Dash, Buddy Feyne, Erskine Hawkins, William Johnson
Twilight Time---Al Nevins, Morty Nevins, Buck Ram
Two Hearts That Pass In the Night---Ernesto Lecuona
What a Difference a Day Made---Maria Grever, Stanley Adams
When You Wish Upon a Star---Leigh Harline, Ned Washington
White Christmas---Irving Berlin
Who Wouldn't Love You? ---Carl Fischer, Bob Carey
Yes Indeed---Sy Oliver
You Always Hurt the One You Love---Doris Fisher, Allan Roberts
You and I---Meredith Willson
You Are My Sunshine---Jimmie Davis, Charles Mitchell
You'd Be So Nice To Come Home To---Cole Porter
You Don't Know What Love Is---Gene De Paul, Don Raye
You'll Never Know---Mack Gordon, Harry Warren

You're Nobody Till Somebody Loves You---James Cavanaugh, Russ Morgan, Larry Stock
Yours---Gonzalo Roig, Albert Gamse
You Stepped Out of a Dream---Nacio Herb Brown, Gus Kahn
You Walk By---Bernie Wayne, Ben Raleigh
You Were Never Lovelier---Jerome Kern, Johnny Mercer

1945-1949

Again---Corcas Cochran, Lionel Newman
All I Want For Christmas (Is My Two Front Teeth)---Don Gardner
All Through the Day---Jerome Kern, Oscar Hammerstein
Almost Like Being In Love---Alan Jay Lerner, Frederick Loewe
Always True To You In My Fashion---Cole Porter
Anniversary Song, The ---Ivanovici, Saul Chaplin, Al Jolson
Anything You Can Do---Irving Berlin
Aren't You Glad You're You? ---Johnny Burke, James Van Heusen
Autumn Serenade---Peter DeRose, Sammy Gallop
A--You're Adorable---Buddy Kaye, Sidney Lippman, Fred Wise
Baby It's Cold Outside---Frank Loesser
Baia (BMI)---Ary Barroso
Bali H'ai---Rodgers and Hammerstein
Ballerina---Bob Russell, Carl Sigman
Ballin' the Jack (BMI)---Chris Smith, Jim Burris
Beyond the Sea---Jack Lawrence, Charles Trenet, Albert Lasry
Bibbidi-Bobbidi-Boo---Mack David, Al Hoffman, Jerry Livingston
Bouquet of Roses (BMI)---Steve Nelson, Robert Hilliard
Bumble Boogie---Rimsky-Korsakov, Jack Fina
But Beautiful---Johnny Burke, James Van Heusen
Buttons and Bows---Ray Evans, Jay Livingston
Bye Bye Baby---Leo Robin, Jule Styne
Caldonia (BMI)---Fleecie Moore
Chequita Banana---Len MacKenzie, Garth Montgomery, William Wirges
Chickery Chick---Sylvia Dee, Sidney Lippman
Civilization (Bongo-Bongo-Bongo)---Robert Hilliard, Carl Sigman
Coffee Song, The ---Robert Hilliard, Dick Miles
Come Closer To Me (BNI)---Osvaldo Farres, Al Steward
Come Rain Or Come Shine---Harold Arlen, Johnny Mercer
Come To the Mardi Gras (BMI)---M. Bulhoes, M. DeOliviera, E. Drake, J. Shirl
Comme Ci-Come Ca---Bruno Coquatrix, Pierre Dudan, Alex Kramer, Joan Whitney
Cool Water (BMI)---Bob Nolan
Cruising Down the River---Eily Beadell, Nell Tollerton
Cuanto Le Gusta (BMI)---Gabriel Ruiz, Ray Gilbert
Day By Day---Sammy Cahn, Axel Stordahl, Paul Weston
Dear Hearts and Gentle People---Sammy Fain, Robert Hilliard
Delilah (BMI)---Jimmy Stirl, Henry Manners
Diamonds Are a Girl's Best Friend---Leo Robin, Jule Styne
Dig You Later (Hubba-Hubba-Hubba)---Harold Adamson, Jimmy McHugh
Doctor, Lawyer, Indian Chief---Hoagy Carmichael, Paul Webster
Doin' What Comes Natur'lly---Irving Berlin
Don't Cry, Joe---Joe Marsala
Dream---Johnny Mercer
Dreamer's Holiday---Kim Gannon, Mabel Wayne
Dream Is a Wish Your Heart Makes, A ---Mack David, Al Hoffman, Jerry Livingston
Early Autumn ---Ralph Burns
Easy Street (BMI)---Alan R. Jones
Enjoy Yourself, It's Later Than You Think---Herb Magidson, Carl Sigman
Far Away Places---Alex Kramer, Joan Whitney
Fellow Needs a Girl, A ---Rodgers and Hammerstein
Feudin' and Fightin'---Al Dubin, Burton Lane
Five Minutes More---Sammy Cahn, Jule Styne
Forever and Ever---Malia Rosa, Franz Winkler

For You, For Me, For Evermore---Gershwin brothers
For Sentimental Reasons---Deke Watson, William Best
Full Moon and Empty Arms---Serge Rachmaninoff, Buddy Kaye, Ted Mossman
Gal In Calico, A ---Leo Robin, Arthur Schwartz
Gentleman Is a Dope, The ---Rodgers and Hammerstein
Girl That I Marry, The ---Irving Berlin
Give Me the Simple Life---Rube Bloom, Harry Ruby
Golden Earrings---Ray Evans, Jay Livingston, Victor Young
Gypsy, The ---Billy Reid
Hair of Gold, Eyes of Blue---Sunny Skylar
Happy Talk---Rodgers and Hammerstein
Haunted Heart---Arthur Schwartz, Howard Dietz
How Are Things In Glocca Morra? ---E. Y. Harburg, Burton Lane
Huckle-Buck---Roy Alfred, Andy Gibson
I Can't Begin To Tell You---Mack Gordon, James Monaco
I Don't Care If the Sun Don't Shine---Mack David
I Don't Know Enough About You (BMI)---kPeggy Lee, Dave Barbour
If I Loved You---Rodgers and Hammerstein
If This Isn't Love--- E. Y. Harburg, Burton Lane
I Got the Sun In the Morning---Irving Berlin
I'll Buy That Dream---Herb Magidson, Allie Wrubel
I'll Close My Eyes---Buddy Kaye, Billy Reid
I Love You For Sentimental Reasons (BMI)---Deke Watson, Alan Best
I'm a Lonely Little Petunia---Maurie Hartman, Billy Faber, Johnny Kamano
I'm Beginning To See the Light---D. Ellington, Don George, Johnny Hodges, Harry James
I'm Gonna Wash That Man Right Outa My Hair---Rodgers and Hammerstein
I'm So Lonesome I Could Cry (BMI)---Hank Williams
In Love In Vain---Jerome Kern, Leo Robin
I Should Care---Sammy Cahn, Axel Stordahl, Paul Weston
I Still Get Jealous---Sammy Cahn, Jule Styne
It Might As Well Be Spring---Rodgers and Hammerstein
It's a Good Day---Dave Barbour, Peggy Lee
It's a Pity To Say Goodnight---Billy Reid
It's Been a Long - Long Time---Sammy Cahn, Jule Styne
It's Magic---Sammy Cahn, Jule Styne
It's You Or No One---Sammy Cahn, Jule Styne
I've Got a Lovely Bunch of Cocoanuts---Fred Heatherton
I Wish I Didn't Love You So---Frank Loesser
I Wonder, I Wonder, I Wonder---Daryl Hutchins
Jersey Bounce, The ---T. Bradshaw, B. Feyne, E. Johnson, B. Plater, R. B. Wright
June Is Bustin' Out All Over---Rodgers and Hammerstein
Laughing On the Outside (Crying On the Inside) (BMI)---Bernie Wayne, Ben Raleigh
Laura---Johnny Mercer, David Raksin
Lavender Blue (Dilly-Dilly)---Eliot Daniel, Larry Morey
La Vie En Rose---Edith Piaf, Mack David, Louiguy
Let It Snow! Let It Snow! Let It Snow! ---Sammy Cahn, Jule Styne
Let's Take an Old-Fashioned Walk---Irving Berlin
Linda---Jack Lawrence
Little Bird Told Me, A---Harvey O. Brooks
Lonely Town---Leonard Bernstein, Betty Comden, Adolf Green
Love---Ralph Blane, Hugh Martin
Love Is Where You Find It---Earl K. Brent, Nacio Herb Brown
Love Letters---Edward Heyman, Victor Young
Lucky To Be Me---Leonard Bernstein, Betty Comden, Adolph Green
Mambo Number Five (BMI)---Perez Prado
Mam'selle---Mack Gordon, Edmund Goulding
Manana (BMI)---Dave Barbour, Peggy Lee
Maybe You'll Be There---Rube Bloom, Sammy Gallop
Misirlou (BMI)---N. Roubanis
Mocking Bird Hill---Vaughan Horton

Mona Lisa---Ray Evans, Jay Livingston
More I See You, The ---Mack Gordon, Harry Warren
Mule Train---Fred Glickman, Hy Heath, Johnny Lange
My Adobe Hacienda (BMI)---Louise Massey, Johnny Warrington, Lee Penny
My Darling, My Darling---Frank Loesser
My Foolish Heart---Ned Washington, Victor Young
My Happiness---Borney Bergantine, Betty Peterson
My Shawl (Ombo) (BMI)---Xavier Cugat, Pedro Berrios, Stanley Adams
Nature Boy---Eden Ahbez
Near You---Francis Craig, Kermit Goell
New York, New York---Leonard Bernstein, Betty Comden, Adolph Green
Night Has a Thousand Eyes, The ---Buddy Bernier, Jerry Brainin
Now Is the Hour---Maewa Kaihau, Clement Scott, Dorothy Stewart
Oh! But I Do---Arthur Schwartz, Leo Robin
Oh! What It Seemed To Be---Bennie Benjamin, Frankie Carl, George Weiss
Old Devil Moon---E.Y. Harburg, Burton Lane
Old Lamp Lighter, The ---Nat Simon, Charlie Tobias
Old Master Painter, The ---Gaven Hillespie, Beasley Smith
Ole Buttermilk Sky---Jack Brooks, Hoagy Carmichael
On a Slow Boat To China---Frank Loesser
Once In Love With Amy---Frank Loesser
On the Acheson, Topeka and Santa Fe---Johnny Mercer, Harry Warren
Open the Door, Richard (BMI)---Don Howell, Jack McVea, John Mason, Dusty Fletcher
Out Of This World---Harold Arlen, Johnny Mercer
Papa, Won't You Dance With Me? ---Sammy Cahn, Jule Styne
Personality---Johnny Burke, James Van Heusen
Pigalle---Charles Newman, Georges Ulmer, Geo Koger
Powder Your Face With Sunshine---Carmen Lombardo, Stanley Rochinski
Red Roses For a Blue Lady---Roy Brodsky, Sid Tepper
Riders In the Sky---Stan Jones
Room Full of Roses (BMI)---Tim Spencer
Rudolph The Red-Nosed Reindeer---Johnny Marks
Rumors Are Flying---Bennie Benjamin, George Weiss
Save the Bones for Henry Jones---UI I p.49
Sentimental Me---Jimmy Cassin, Jim Morehead
Serenade Of the Bells---Al Goodhart, Kay Twomey, Al Urbano
She Wore a Yellow Ribbon (BMI)---M. Ottiner
Shoofly Pie and Apple Pan Dowdy---Sammy Gallop, Guy Wood
Sioux City Sue---Roy Freedman, Dick Thomas
Smoke! Smoke! Smoke that Cigarette (BMI)---Merle Travis, Tex Williams
So In Love---Cole Porter
Someday You'll Want Me To Want You (BMI)---Jimmy Hodges
Some Enchanted Evening---Rodgers and Hammerstein
Some Sunday Morning---Ray Heindorf, M. K. Jerome, Ted Koehler
South America, Take It Away---Harold Rome
Stanley Steamer, The ---Ralph Blane, Harry Warren
Stella By Starlight---Ned Washington, Victor Young
Stepping Out With My Baby---Irving Berlin
Sunday Kind of Love, A---Barbara Belle, Anita Leonard, Louis Prima, Stan Rhodes
Surrender---Bennie Benjamin, George Weiss
Symphony---Alex Alstone, Jack Lawrence
Take It Away (BMI)---Albert Gamse, Enrique Madriguera
Tenderly---Walter Gross, Jack Lawrence
That Lucky Old Sun---Haven Gillespie, Beasley Smith
That's For Me---Rodgers and Hammerstein
There Is Nothing Like a Dame---Rodgers and Hammerstein
There's No Business Like Show Business---Irving Berlin
There's No Tomorrow (O Solo Mio)---Leon Carr, Leo Corday, Al Hoffman
They Say It's Wonderful---Irving Berlin
Things We Did Last Summer, The ---Sammy Cahn, Jule Styne

Third Man Theme, The ---Anton Karas
This Nearly Was Mine---Rodgers and Hammerstein
Till the End Of Time---Frederick Chopin, Buddy Kaye, Ted Mossman
To Each His Own---Ray Evans, Lay Livingston
Too Fat Polka---Ross MacLean, Arthur Richardson
Tree Grows In the Meadow, A ---Billy Reid
We'll Be Together Again---Carl Fisher
When I'm Not Near the Girl I Love---E.Y. Harburg, Burton Lane
While We're Young (BMI)---Alec Wilder, Morty Palitz, William Engvick
Whole World Is Singing My Song, The ---Maun Curtis, Vic Mizzy
Why Can't You Behave? ---Cole Porter
Wonderful Guy, A ---Rodgers and Hammerstein
Woody Woodpecker---Ramiz Idriss, George Tibbles
Wunderbar---Cole Porter
You Belong To My Heart (BMI)---Agustin Lara, Ray Gilbert
You Call Everybody Darling---Sam Martin, Ben Trace, Clem Watts
You Can't Be True, Dear---Hal Cotton, Gerhard Ebeler, Hans Otten
You Keep Coming Back Like a Song---Irving Berlin
You'll Never Walk Alone---Rodgers and Hammerstein
You Make Me Feel So Young---Mack Gordon, Josef Myrow
Younger Than Springtime---Rodgers and Hammerstein
You're Breaking My Heart (BMI)---Leoncavallo, Pat Genaro, Sunny Skylar
You're My Thrill---Jay Gorney, Sidney Clare
Zip-a-Dee-Doo-Dah---Ray Gilbert, Allie Wrubel

1950-1954

Adios---Enrique Madriguera, C. R. Del Campo, M. Woods
Again (BMI)---Lionel Newman, Dorcas Cochran
Allez-Vous-En, Go Away---Cole Porter
All My Love---Henri Contet, Mitchell Parish, Paul Durand
All Of You---Cole Porter
And So To Sleep Again---Joe Marsala, Sunny Skylar
And This Is My Beloved---Alexander Borodin, George Forrest, Robert Wright
Answer Me (My Love)---Fred Rauch, Carl Sigman, Gerhard Winkler
Anytime (BMI)---Herbert Happy Lawson
Anywhere I Wander---Frank Loesser
April In Portugal---Paul Ferrao, Jimmy Kennedy
Arrivederci Roma---R. Rascel
Auf Wiederseh'n Sweetheart (BMI)---Eberhard Storch, John Turner, John Sexton
Baubles, Bangles and Beads---Alexander Borodin, George Forrest, Robert Wright
Be Anything (But Be Mine)---Irving Gordon
Beautiful Brown Eyes (BMI)---Arthur Smith, Alton Delmore, Jerry Capehart
Because Of You (BMI)---Arthur Hammerstein, Dudley Wilkerson
Because You're Mine---Sammy Cahn, Nicholas Brodszky
Belle Of the Ball ---Leroy Anderson, Mitchell Parish
Be My Life's Companion---Milton DeLugg, Robert Hilliard
Be My Love---Nicholas Brodszky, Sammy Cahn
Blacksmith Blues (BMI)---Jack Holmes
Blue Gardenia---Bob Russell, Lester Lee
Blue Tango---Leroy Anderson, Mitchell Parish
Blue Velvet---Bernie Wayne, Lee Morris
Botch-a-Me (BMI)---Eddie Y. Stanley, R. Morbelli, I. Astore
Bunny Hop (BMI)---Ray Anthony, Leonard Aulette
Bushel and a Peck, A ---Frank Loesser
Cara Mia ---Lee Lange, Tulio Trapani
C'est Magnifique---Cole Porter
C'est Si Bon---Andre Hornez, Jerry Seelen, Henri Betti
Chattanooga Shoe Shine Boy (BMI)---Harry Stone, Jack Stapp
Cold - Cold Heart (BMI)---Hank Williams
Come On-a My House (BMI)---William Saroyan, Ross Bagdasarian

Count Your Blessings Instead of Sheep---Irving Berlin
Count Every Star---Sammy Gallop, Bruno Coquatrix
Cross Over the Bridge---Bennie Benjamin, George Weiss
Crying In the Chapel (BMI)---Artie Glenn
Cry Of the Wild Goose (BMI)---Terry Gilkyson
Dansero (BMI)---Richard Hayman, Sol Parker, Elliot Daniels
Dearie---Robert Hilliard, Dave Mann
Delicado---Waldyr Azevado, Jack Lawrence
Domino---Jack Plante, Don Raye, Louis Ferrari
Don't Ya Go Away Mad---Jimmy Mundy, Illinois Jacquet, Al Stillman
Don't Let the Stars Get In Your Eyes (BMI)---Slim Willet
Ebbtide---Robert Maxwell, Carl Sigman
Eh Cumpari (BMI)---Julius LaRosa, Archie Bleyer
End Of a Love Affair, The (BMI)---Edward C. Redding
Fanny---Harold Rome
Fascination---Dick Manning, F.D. Marchetti
Fly Me To the Moon (In other words)---Bart Howard
From Here To Eternity---Fred Karger, Bob Wells
From This Moment On---Cole Porter
Frosty the Snowman---Steve Nelson, J. Rollins
Getting To Know You---Rodgers and Hammerstein
Glow Worm (BMI)---Paul Lincke, Lilla Ribinson, Johnny Mercer (from 1902)
Gone Fishin'---Charles and Nick Kenny
Gonna Get Along Without Ya Now---Milton Kellen
Goodnight, Irene (BMI)---Huddie Ledbetter, John Lomax
Half As Much (BMI)---Hank Williams
Happy Wanderer, The --- Floren Siegesmund, Antonia Ridge, F.W. Moller
Hello, Young Lovers---Rodgers and Hammerstein
Here In My Arms (BMI)---Pat Genaro, Lou Levinson, Bill Borrelli
Hernando's Hideaway---Richard Adler, Jerry Ross
Hey, Good Lookin'---Hank Williams
Hey There---Richard Adler, Jerry Ross
High and Mighty, The ---Dimitri Tiomkin, Ned Washington
High Noon ---Dimitri Tiomkin, Ned Washington
Hi Lili--Hi Lo---Helen Deutsch, Branislau Kaper
Hold Me-Hold Me-Hold Me---Betty Comden, Adolph Green, Jule Styne
Home For the Holidays---Robert Allen, Al Stillman
Hoop-Dee-Doo---Milton DeLugg, Frank Loesser
How Do You Speak To An Angel? ---Robert Hilliard, Jule Styne
How Much Is that Doggie In the Window? ---Bob Merrill
I Believe---Ervin Drake, Irvin Graham, Jimmy Shirl, Al Stillman
If I Give My Heart To You---Jimmy Brewster, Jimmie Crane, Al Jacobs
If I Knew You Were Coming I'd've Baked a Cake---Al Hoffman, Bob Merrill, Clem Watts
If I Were a Bell---Frank Loesser
If You Loved Me (BMI)---Marguerite Monnot, Geoffrey Parsons
I Get Ideas When I Dance With You (BMI)---Dorcas Cochran, Lenny Danders
I'll Never Be Free---Bennie Benjamin, George Weiss
I Love Paris---Cole Porter
I Left My Heart In San Francisco---George Cory, Douglass Cross
I'm Hans Christian Andersen---Frank Loesser
I'm Walking Behind You---Billy Reid
I'm Yours (BMI)---Robert Mellin
In the Cool-Cool-Cool Of the Evening---Hoagy Carmichael, Johnny Mercer
I Saw Mommy Kissing Santa Claus---Tommy Connor
Istanbul (Not Constantinople)---Jimmy Kennedy, Nat Simon
I Talk To the Trees---Lerner and Loewe
I Taut I Taw a Puddycat---Warren Foster, Alan Livingston, Billy May
It's a Lazy Afternoon---Jerome Moross, John LaTouche
It's All In the Game---Charles G. Dawes, Carl Sigman (from 1912)
It's All Right With Me---Cole Porter

It's a Lovely Day Today---Irving Berlin
It's So Nice To Have a Man Around the House---Jack Elliot, Harold Spina
I've Never Been In Love Before---Frank Loesser
I Went To Your Wedding (BMI)---Jessie Mae Robinson
I Whistle a Happy Tune---Rodgers and Hammerstein
Jambalaya (BMI)---Hank Williams
Jezebel---Wayne Shanklin
Just Another Polka---Milton DeLugg, Frank Loesser
Keep It a Secret---Jessie Mae Robinson
Keep It Gay---Rodgers and Hammerstein
Kiss of Fire (BMI)---Lester Allen, Robert Hill
Kiss To Build a Dream On, A---Bert Kalmar, Harry Ruby, Oscar Hammerstein
Let Me Go, Lover---Jenny Lou Carson, Al Hill
Limelight---Charlie Chaplin
Lion Sleeps Tonight, The (a-Wimoweh) (BMI)---P. Campbell, H. Paretti and 4 others
Lisbon Antigua---Harry Dupree, Jose Galhardo, Paul Portela and others
Little Shoemaker, The---Francis Lemarque, W. Geoffrey Parsons and others
Little Things Mean a Lot---Edith Lindeman, Carl Stutz
Little White Cloud That Cried, The ---Johnnie Ray
Lost In Loveliness---Leo Robin, Sigmund Romberg, Don Walker
Love Is a Simple Thing---June Carroll, Arthur Siegel
Loveliest Night Of the Year, The ---J. Rosas, Irving Aaronson, Paul F. Webster
Luck Be a Lady---Frank Loesser
Lullaby of Birdland (BMI)---George Shearing, George Weiss
Make Love To Me---George Grunies, Allan Copeland and others
Make Yourself Comfortable---Bob Merrill
Man That Got Away, The ---Harold Arlen, Ira Gershwin
Many Times (BMI)---Jessie Barnes, Felix Stahl
Marshmallow World---Peter DeRose, Carl Sigman
May the Good Lord Bless and Keep You---Meredith Willson
Melody Of Love ---H. Englemann, Tom Glazer
Mister and Mississippi---Irving Gordon
Mister Sandman---Pat Ballard
Mockin' Bird Hill---Vaughn Horton
Morningside Of the Mountain, The ---Dick Manning, Larry Stock
Music! Music! Music! ---Bernie Baum, Stephan Weiss
My Heart Cries For You---Percy Faith, Carl Sigman
My Truly - Truly Fair---Bob Merrill
Naughty Lady of Shady Lane, The ---Roy C. Bennett, Sid Tepper
Night Train (BMI)---Jimmy Forrest, Oscar Washington, Lewis C. Simpkins
No Other Love---Rodgers and Hammerstein
No Two People---Frank Loesser
Oh Happy Day---Don Howard, Nancy Binns Reed
Oh Mein Papa---Paul Burkhard, Geoffrey Parsons, John Turner
Old Piano Roll Blues, The ---Cy Coben
Orange Colored Sky---Milton Delugg, Willie Stein
Papa Loves Mambo---Al Hoffman, Dick Manning, Bix Reichner
Petite Waltz, The (BMI)---Phyllis Claire, Hoe Heyne, E.A. Ellington
Pittsburgh, Pennsylvania---Bob Merrill
Please, Mr. Sun (BMI)---Ray Getzov, Sid Frank
Pretend---Dan Belloc, Lew Douglas and others
Rag Mop (BMI)---Johnnie Lee Wills, Deacon Anderson
Rags To Riches---Richard Adler, Jerry Ross
Richochet (BMI)---Larry Coleman, Joe Darion, Norman Gimbel
Rock Around the Clock---Jimmy DeKnight, Max C. Freedman
Ruby---Mitchell Parish, Heinz Roemheld
Sam's Song---Jack Elliot, Lew Quadling
Secret Love---Sammy Fain, Paul F. Webster
Serenata---Leroy Anderson, Mitchell Parish
Shanghai---Milton DeLugg, Robert Hilliard

Sh-boom, Life Could Be a Dream (BMI)---Claude Feaster, Carl Feaster and others
Shrimp Boats---Paul Mason Howard, Paul Weston
Sin (It's No)---Chester R. Shull, George Hoven
Sit Down, You're Rockin' the Boat---Frank Loesser
Skokiaan ---Tom Glazer, August Musarurgwa
Sleigh Ride---Leroy Anderson, Mitchell Parish
Slowpoke (BMI)---Frank (PeeWee) King, Redd Stewart, Chilton Price
Smile---Charlie Chaplin, Geoffrey Parsons, John Turner
Somewhere Along the Way---Kurt Adams (James Van Heusen), Sammy Gallop
Sound Off!---Willie Lee Duckworth, Bernie Lentz
Sparrow In the Treetop---Bob Merrill
Steam Heat---Richard Adler, Jerry Ross
Stranger In Paradise, A ---A. Borodin, George Forrest, Robert Wright
Sway (BMI)---Norman Gimbel, Pablo Ruiz
Sweet Violets---Cy Coben, Charles Grean
Teach Me Tonight---Sammy Cahn, Gene DePaul
Tell Me Why (BMI)---Marty Gold, Al Alberts
Tennessee Waltz, The (BMI)---PeeWee King, Redd Stewart
That's All (BMI)---Bob Haymes, Alan Brandt
That's Amore---Jack Brooks, Harry Warren
That's Entertainment---Howard Dietz, Arthur Schwartz
There's No Place Like Home For the Holidays---Robert Allen, Al Stillman
They Call the Wind Maria---Lerner and Loewe
Thing, The (BMI)---Charles Grean
This Ole House --- Stuart Hamblen
Three Coins In the Fountain---Sammy Cahn, Jule Styne
Thumbelina---Frank Loesser
Till I Waltz Again With You---Sidney Prosen
Too Young---Sylvia Dee, Sid Lippman
Tzema – Tzena - Tzena---Issachar Miron, Mitchell Parish
Under Paris Skies---Jean Drejac, Kim Gannon, Hubert Hiraud
Unforgettable---Irving Gordon
Vanessa---Bernie Wayne
Vaya Con Dios---Carl Hoff, Inez James, Buddy Pepper, Larry Russell
Wanted---Jack Fulton, Lois Steele
We Kiss In a Shadow---Rodgers and Hammerstein
We'll Build a Bungalow (BMI)---Betty Bryant, Smalls Mayhams
Wheel of Fortune---Bennie Benjamin, George Weiss
When I Fall In Love---Edward Heyman, Victor Young
Where Is Your Heart? ---Georges Auric, William Engvick
Why Don't You Believe Me? ---Lew Douglas, King Laney, Roy Rodde
Wish You Were Here ---Harold Rome
With These Hands---Benny Davis, Abner Silver
Wonderful Copenhagen---Frank Loesser
Would I Love You (Love You, Love You?) ---Bob Russell, Harold Spina
You Belong To Me (BMI)---Chilton Price, PeeWee King, Redd Stewart
Young and Foolish---Albert Hague, Arnold Horwitt
Young At Heart (BMI)---Johnny Richards, Carolyn Leigh
Your Cheatin' Heart (BMI)---Hank Williams
You're Just In Love---Irving Berlin
You, You, You---Lotar Olias, Robert Mallin

1955-1959

Adventures In Paradise (Theme from)---Dorcas Cochran, Lionel Newman
Ain't That a Shame? (BMI)---Dave Bartholomeo, Fats Domino
All At Once You Love Her---Rodgers and Hammerstein
Allegheny Moon---Al Hoffman, Dick Manning
All Shook Up (BMI)---Otis Blackwell, Elvis Presley
All the Way---Sammy Cahn, James Van Heusen
An Affair To Remember---Harold Adamson, Leo McCarey, Harry Warren

Anastasia---Alfred Newman, Paul F. Webster
April Love---Sammy Fain, Paul F. Webster
Around the World---Harold Adamson, Victor Young
Autumn Leaves---Jacques Prevert, Johnny Mercer, Joseph Kosma
Ballad Of Davy Crockett (BMI)---Tom Blackburn, George Bruns
Banana Boat Song (BMI)---Alan Arkus, Bob Carey, Erik Darling
Be-Bop-a-Lua (BMI)---Gene Vincent, Tex Davis
Best Of Everything, The ---Sammy Cahn, Alfred Newman
Bible Tells Me So, The ---Dale Evans
Blossom Fell, A ---Howard Barnes, Harold Cornelius, Dominic John
Blue Star---Edward Heyman, Victor Young
Broken-Hearted Melody---Hal David, Sherman Edwards
Butterfly---Bernie Lowe, Kal Mann
Bye-Bye Love (BMI)---Felice Bryant, Boudleaux Bryant
Ca, C'est L'amour---Cole Porter
Canadian Sunset (BMI)---Eddie Heywood, Norman Gimbel
Catch a Falling Star---Lee Pockriss, Paul Vance
Certain Smile, A ---Sammy Fain, Paul Francis Webster
Chances Are---Robert Allen, Al Stillman
Chanson d'amour---Wayne Shanklin
Cherry Pink and Apple Blossom White---Mack David, Louiguy
Children's Marching Song---Traditional and Malcolm Arnold
Climb Every Mountain---Rodgers and Hammerstein
Come Dance With Me---James Van Heusen, Sammy Cahn
Cry Me a River---Arthur Hamilton
Diana (BMI)---Paul Anka
Do I Love You (Beacuse You're Beautiful)? ---Rodgers and Hammerstein
Don't You Know? (Musetta's Waltz)---G. Puccini, Bobby Worth
Do-Re-Mi---Rodgers and Hammerstein
Everybody Loves a Lover---Richard Adler, Robert Allen
Everything's Coming Up Roses---Stephen Sondheim, Jule Styne
Fever (BMI)---John Davenport, Eddie Cooley
For the First Time ---M. Panzeri, Buck Ram and others
Get Me To the Church On Time---Lerner and Loewe
Gidget---Pattie Washington, Fred Karger
Gigi---Lerner and Loewe
Go Chase a Moonbeam---Lee Pockriss, Paul J. Vance
Great Pretender, The ---Buck Ram
Hawaiian Wedding Song---Al Hoffman, Dick Manning
He---Jack Richards, Richard Mullan
Heart---Richard Adler, Jerry Ross
Hey! Jealous Lover---Sammy Cahn, Kay Twomey, Bee Walker
High Hopes---Sammy Cahn, James Van Heusen
Honeycomb---Bob Merrill
Hot Diggity--- A. Emmanuel Chabrier, Al Hoffman, Dick Manning
(How Little It Matters) How Little We Know---Carolyn Leigh, Philip Springer
I Can't Stop Loving You---Don Gibson
I Could Have Danced All Night---Lerner and Loewe
I Enjoying Being a Girl---Rodgers and Hammerstein
I Feel Pretty---Stephen Sondheim and Leonard Bernstein
I Know, I Know---Edith Lindemann, Carl Stutz
I'll Never Stop Loving You---Nicholas Brodszky, Sammy Cahn
I'm Glad I'm Not Young Anymore---Lerner and Loewe
Impossible---Steve Allen
I Remember It Well---Lerner and Loewe
It's Not For Me To Say---Robert Allen, Al Stillman
I've Grown Accustomed To Her Face---Lerner and Loewe
I Walk the Line---Johnny Cash
I Wanna Be Around---Johnny Mercer, Sadie Vimmerstedt
Just Because---Lloyd Price

Just In Time---Betty Comden, Adolph Green, Jule Styne
Kansas City---Jerry Leiber, Mike Stoller
Learning the Blues---Delores Vicki Silvers
Lida Rose---Meredith Willson
Liechtensteiner Polka---Ed. Kotscher, R. Lindt
Like Young---Paul F. Webster, Andre Previn
Lil' Darlin'---Neal Hefti
Longest Walk, The ---Eddie Pola, Fred Spielman
Love and Marriage---Sammy Cahn, James Van Heusen
Love Is a Many Splendored Thing---Sammy Fain, Paul F. Webster
Love, Look Away---Rodgers and Hammerstein
Love Me Tender (BNI)---George Poulton, Elvis Presley, Vera Matson
Mack the Knife---Marc Blitzstein, Bertold Brecht, Kurt Weill (from 1928)
Magic Moments---Burt Bacharach, Hal David
Mangoes---Sid Wayne, Dee Libbey
Maria---Stephen Sondheim, Leonard Bernstein
Marianne---Terry Gilkyson, Frank Miller, Richard Dehr
Married I Can Always Get---Gordon Jenkins
Matilda---Norman Span
Melodie D'amour---Jimmy Phillips, Marcel Stellman, Henri Salvador
Memories Are Made Of This---Terry Gilkyson, Richard Dehr, Frank Miller
Misty---Johnny Burke, Erroll Garner
Moments To Remember---Robert Allen, Al Stillman
Mr. Wonderful---Jerry Bock (BMI), Larry Holofcener, George Weiss
Mutual Admiration Society---Matt Dubey, Harold Karr
My Favorite Things---Rodgers and Hammerstein
My Heart Reminds Me---C. Bargani, Al Stillman
My Prayer---Georges Boulanger, Jimmy Kennedy
Night They Invented Champagne, The ---Lerner and Loewe
Non Dimenticar (BMI)---Shelley Dobbins, P. G. Redi, Michelle Galdieri
No, Not Much ---Robert Allen, Al Stillman
Nothing Ever Changes My Love For You---Marvin Fisher, Jack Segal
Old Cape Cod---Claire Rothrock, Milt Yakus, Allan Jeffrey
On the Street Where You Live---Lerner and Loewe
Party's Over, The ---Betty Comden, Adolph Green, Jule Styne
Pete Kelly's Blues---Sammy Cahn, Ray Heindorf
Picnic---George Duning, Steve Allen
Pillow Talk -- Inez James, Buddy Pepper
Poor People of Paris, The ---Rene Rouzaud, Jack Lawrence, Marguerite Monnot
Primrose Lane---George Callender, Wayne Shanklin
Put Your Head On My Shoulder (BMI)---Paul Anka
Quiet Village (BMI)---Leslie Baxter
Rain In Spain, The ---Lerner and Loewe
Return To Me---Danny Di Minno, Carmen Lombardo
Satin Doll---Johnny Mercer, Billy Strayhorn, Duke Ellington
Seventy-Six Trombones---Meredith Willson
Singing the Blues (BMI)---Melvin Endsley
Sixteen Tons (BMI)---Merle Travis
Small World---Stephen Sondheim, Jule Styne
Soft Summer Breeze (BMI)---Eddie Heywood, Judy Spencer
Somebody Up There Likes Me---Sammy Cahn, Bronislau Kaper
Something's Coming---Stephen Sondheim and Leonard Bernstein
Something's Gotta Give---Johnny Mercer
Song Of Raintree County, The ---Johnny Green, Paul F. Webster
Standing On the Corner---Frank Loesser
Strange Are the Ways of Love---Dimitri Tiomkin, Ned Washington
Suddenly There's a Valley (BMI)---Chuck Meyer, Biff Jones
Summer Place. A (theme from)---Max Steiner, Mack Discant
Sunday In New York---Portia Nelson
Sweet and Gentle (BMI)---George Thorn, Otilio Portal

Swingin' Shepherd Blues (BMI)---Moe Koffman
Tammy---Ray Evans, Jay Livingston
Tender Trap, The ---Sammy Cahn, James Van Heusen
Tequila (BMI)---Chuck Rio
Thank Heaven For Little Girls---Lerner and Loewe
Thee I Love (theme: Friendly Persuasion)---Dimitri Tiomkin, Paul F. Webster
This Could Be the Start Of Something Big---Steve Allen
This Is All I Ask---Gordon Jenkins
Till---Pierre Buisson, Charles Danvers, Carl Sigman
Till There Was You---Meredith Willson
Too Close For Comfort---Jerry Bock (BMI), Jerry Holofcener, George Weiss
True Love---Cole Porter
Two Different Worlds ---Al Fresch, Sid Wayne
Two Lost Souls---Richard Adler, Jerry Ross
Unchained Melody---Alex North, Hy Zaret
Venus ---Ed Marshall
Very Precious Love, A ---Sammy Fain, Paul F. Webster
Volare ---Domenico Modugno, F. Migliacci, Mitchell Parish
Wake the Town and Tell the People---Sammy Gallop, Jerry Livingston
Wayward Wind, The ---Herb Newman, Stan Lebowsky
Whatever Lola Wants, Lola Gets---Richard Adler, Jerry Ross
Whatever Will Be, Will Be (Que Sera Sera)---Ray Evans, Jay Livingston
When Sunny Gets Blue---Jack Segal, Marvin Fisher
When You're In Love---Maxwell Anderson, Arthur Schwartz
Wild Is the Wind---Dimitri Tiomkin, Ned Washington
Witchcraft--- Cy Coleman, Carolyn Leigh
With a Little Bit Of Luck---Lerner and Loewe
Wouldn't It Be Loverly?---Lerner and Loewe
Yellow Bird---Alan Bergman, Marilyn Keith, Norman Luboff
Yellow Rose of Texas, The ---Don George
You Are Beautiful---Rodgers and Hammerstein
You Are Never Far Away From Me---Robert Allen
Young and Warm and Wonderful---Lou Singer, Hy Zaret
Young Love (BMI)---Carole Johner, Ric Cartey

1960-1964

Al-Di-La---Carlo Donida, Erwin Drake, Mogol
Alley Cat (BMI)---Frank Bjorn
All Over the World---Al Frisch, Charles Tobias
Almost There---Jerry Keller, Gloria Shayne
As Long As He Needs Me---Lionel Bart
As Tears Go By---Mick Jagger, Andrew Oldham, Keith Richard
Baby Elephant Walk---Henry Mancini
Big Girls Don't Cry---Bob Crewe, Bob Gaudio
Blame It On the Bossa Nova (BMI)---Barry Mann, Cynthia Weil
Blowin' In the Wind---Bob Dylan
Blue On Blue---Burt Bacharach, Hal David
Bluesette---Jean (Toots) Thielemans and Norman Gimble
Breaking Up Is Hard To Do (BMI)---Neil Sedaka, Howard Greenfield
Calcutta---Hans Bradtke, Paul Vance, Lee Pockriss, Heino Gaze
Call Me Irresponsible---Sammy Cahn, James Van Heusen
Camelot---Lerner and Loewe
Can't Buy Me Love (BMI)---Lennon and McCartney
Can't Get Over the Bossa Nova ---Marilyn Gins, Eydie Gorme, Steve Lawrence
Can't Help Falling In Love With You---Luigi Creatore, Hugo Perette, George Weiss
Charade---Henry Mancini, Johnny Mercer
Comes Once In a Lifetime---Betty Comden, Adolph Green, Jule Styne
Danke Schoen (BMI)---Bert Kaempfert, Kurt Schwabach, Milt Gabler
Days of Wine and Roses, The ---Henry Mancini, Johnny Mercer
Dear Heart---Ray Evans, Jay Livingston, Henry Mancini

Delaware---Irving Gordon
Dominique---Soeur Sourire, Noel Regnez
Downtown---Tony Hatch
Do You Want To Know a Secret? (BMI)---Lennon and McCartney
(Down By the Station) Early In the Morning (BMI)---Bruce Belland, Glen Larson
Everybody Loves Somebody---Ken Lane, Irving Taylor
Exodus---Ernest Gold
Fly Me To the Moon (In Other Words) (BMI)---Bart Howard
Follow Me---Lerner and Loewe
Funny Girl---Bob Merrill, Jule Styne
Gentle Rain---Luiz Bonfa
Girl from Ipanema, The ---Antonio Carlos Jobim, Norman Gimbel
Good Life, The ---Sacha Distel, Jack Reardon
Green Leaves Of Summer, The   Dimitri Tiomkin, Paul F. Webster
Go Away Little Girl (BMI)---Carol King, Gerry Goffin
Goin' Out Of My Head (BMI)---Teddy Randazzo, Bobby Weinstein
Good Life, The ---Sacha Distel, Jack Reardon
Hard Day's Night, A ---Lennon and McCartney
Hello Dolly---Jerry Herman
Hey, Look Me Over---Cy Coleman, Carolyn Leigh
Hit the Road, Jack (BMI)---Percy Mayfield
Hush – Hush, Sweet Charlotte---Mack David, Frank DeVol
I Ain't Down Yet---Meredith Willson
I Believe In You---Frank Loesser
If Ever I Should Leave You---Lerner and Loewe
If I Had a Hammer (BMI)---Lee Hays, Pete Seeger
I Love You (BMI)---Lennon and McCartney
I'm All Smiles --- Herbert Martin, Michael Leonard
It's a Mad Mad – Mad - Mad World---Mack David, Ernest Gold
Itsy Bitsy Teenie Weenie Yellow Polka Dot Bikini---Lee Pockriss, Paul J. Vance
I Want To Be With You---Lee Adams, Charles Strouse
I Want To Hold Your Hand (BMI)---Lennon and McCartney
I Wish You Love---Albert Beach, Charles Trenet
Java (BMI)---Allen Toussaint, Alvin Tyler, Murray Sporn, Marilyn Schack
Kids---Lee Adams, Charles Strouse
Let It Be Me---Pierre Delanoe, Mann Curtis, Gilbert Becaud
Little Boat (O Barquinho)---Roberto Menescal, Buddy Kaye
Lollipops and Roses---Tony Velona
Love Makes the World Go 'Round---Bob Merrill
Love Me With All Your Heart (BMI)---C. Rigual, M. Rigual, S. Skylar, C. Martiloni
Love With the Proper Stranger---Elmer Bernstein, Johnny Mercer
Make It Easy On Yourself---Burt Bacharach, Hal David
Make Someone Happy---Betty Comden, Adolph Green, Jule Styne
Man Who Shot Liberty Valance, The ---Burt Bacharach, Hal David
Midnight In Moscow (BMI)---Kenny Ball
Moon River---Henry Mancini, Johnny Mercer
More (BMI)---Riz Ortolani, Norman Newell, Nino Oliviero, M. Ciorciolini
Mr. Lucky---Ray Evans, Jay Livingston, Henry Mancini
My Coloring Book (BMI)---John Kander, Frederick Ebb
My Kind Of Girl---Leslie Bricusse
My Kind of Town---Sammy Cahn James Van Heusen
Never On Sunday (BMI)---Manos Hadjidakis, Billy Towne
Nice 'n' Easy---Lew Spence, Marilyn & Alan Bergman
No Strings---Richard Rodgers
On Broadway (BMI)---Barry Mann, Cynthia Weil, Jerry Leiber, Mike Stoller
Once Upon a Time---Lee Adams, Charles Strouse
One Boy---Lee Adams, Charles Strouse
Our Day Will Come---Mort Garson, Robert Hilliard
People---Bob Merrill, Jule Styne
Pink Panther, The ---Henry Mancini

Pocketful of Miracles---Sammy Cahn, James Van Heusen
Puff, the Magic Dragon---Leonard Lipton, Peter Yarrow
Put On a Happy Face---Lee Adams, Charles Strouse
Ramblin' Rose (BMI)---Joe Sherman, Noel Sherman
Release Me (BMI)---Eddie Miller, W. S. Stevenson
Return To Sender (BMI)---Otis Blackwell, Winfield Scott
Ricada Bossa Nova---Luiz Antonio, Djalma Ferreira
Roses are Red, My Love---Al Byron, Paul Evans
Sealed With a Kiss---Gary Geld, Peter Udell
Second Time Around, The ---Sammy Cahn, James Van Heusen
Seventh Dawn, The ---Riziero Ortolani, Paul F. Webster
Softly As I Leave You ---G. Calabrese, Hal Shaper, A. DeVita
So Long, Dearie---Jerry Herman
Stranger On the Shore (BMI)---Robert Mellin, Acker Bilk
Stripper, The ---David Rose
Sweetest Sounds, The ---Richard Rodgers
Taste Of Honey, A ---Ric Maslow, Bobby Scott
Tender Is the Night---Sammy Fain, Paul F. Webster
That's Life---Dean Kay, Kelly Gordon
That Sunday That Summer---Joe Sherman, George D. Weiss
Those Lazy, Hazy, Crazy Days Of Summer---Hans Carste, Charles Tobias
Today---Randy Sparks
Town Without Pity, A ---Dimitri Tiomkin, Ned Washington
Try To Remember---Tom Jones, Harvey Schmidt
Twist, The (BMI)---Hank Ballard
Walk On By---Burt Bacharach, Hal David
Walk On the Wild Side---Elmer Bernstein, Mack David
Walk Right In (BMI)---Erik Darling, Willard Svanbe, Hosie Woods, Gus Cannon
Watermelon Man (BMI)---Herbie Hancock
We'll Sing In the Sunshine---Gale Garnett
Where the Boys Are (BMI)---Howard Greenfield, Neil Sedaka
Why Did I Choose You? ---Michael Leonard, Herbert Martin
Wipe Out (BMI)---Ron Wilson, James Fuller and others
Wives and Lovers---Burt Bacharach, Hal David
Wonderful Day Like Today, A ---Leslie Bricusse, Anthony Newley
Wonderland By Night (BMI)---Klauss Gunter Naiman, Lincoln Chase
Wooden Heart---Fred Wise, Ben Weisman, Berthold Kaempfert, Kay Twomey
You Don't Know Me (BMI)---Cindy Walker, Eddy Arnold
You'll Never Get To Heaven---Burt Bacharach, Hal David

1965-1969

Alfie---Burt Bacharach, Hal David
All---Nino Oliviero, D. Colarossi, M. Grudeff, R. Jessel
All You Need Is Love (BMI)---Lennon and McCartney
And Roses, and Roses---Dorival Caymmi, Ray Gilbert
Aquarius---Galt Mac Dermot, James Rado, Gerome Ragni
Ballad Of the Green Berets---Robin Moore, Barry Sadler
Batman theme---Neil Hefti
Beat Goes On, The (BMI)---Sonny Bono
Big Spender---Cy Coleman, Dorothy Fields
Born Free (BMI)---John Barry, Don Black
Both Sides Now (BMI)---Joni Mitchell
Boy Named Sue, A (BMI)---Skel Silverstein
By the Time I Get To Phoenix (BMI)---Jimmy Webb
Cabaret (BMI)---John Kander, Frederick Ebb
California Dreamin'---John Phillips, Mitchell Phillips
Call Me (BMI)---Tony Hatch
Can't Take My Eyes Off Of You (BMI)---Bob Crewe, Bob Gaudio
Casino Royale theme---Burt Bacharach and Hal David
Cast Your Fate To the Wind (BMI)---Vincent Guaraldi

Cherish (BMI)---Terry Kirkman

Chitty Chitty Bang Bang (BMI)---Richard & Robert Sherman

Classical Gas (BMI)---Mason Williams

Come Saturday Morning---Fred Karlin, Dory Langdon Previn

Daddy Sang Bass (BMI)---Carl Perkins

Daydream---John Sebastian

Day In the Life Of a Fool, A ---Antonio Maria, Francois Lienas, Carl Sigman, Luiz Bonfa

Day Tripper (BMI)---Lennon and McCartney

Didn't We? ---Jimmy Webb

Downtown---Tony Hatch

Sitting On the Dock Of the Bay (BMI)---Otis Redding, Steve Cropper

Do I Hear a Waltz? ---Rodgers and Sondheim

Don't Sleep In the Subway (BMI)---Tony Hatch, Jackie Trent

Do You Know the Way To San Jose?---Burt Bacharach and Hal David

Emily---John Mandel, Johnny Mercer

Everybody Has the Right To Be Wrong---Sammy Cahn, James Van Heusen

Everything Is Beautiful (BMI)---Ray Stevens

Eyes of Love, The ---Quincy Jones, Bob Russell

Feelin' Groovy (BMI)---Paul Simon

Fool On the Hill, The (BMI)---Lennon and McCartney

Forget Domani ---Norman Newell, Riz Ortolani

For Once In My Life---Ronald Miller, Orlando Murden

Galveston---Jimmy Webb

Games People Play (BMI)---Joe South

Gentle On My Mind (BMI)---John Hartford

Georgy Girl---Jim Dale, Tom Springfield

Get Back (BNI)---Lennon and McCartney

Goldfinger (BMI)---John Barry, Leslie Bricusse, Anthony Newley

Goodbye, Charlie---Dory Langdon, Andre Previn

Goodmorning, Starshine---Galt MacDermot, James Rado, Gerome Ragni

Green Green Grass Of Home (BMI)---Curly Putnam

Guantanamera (BMI)---Pete Seeger, Hector Angulo

Harper Valley P.T.A. (BMI)---Tom T. Hall

He Ain't Heavy-He's My Brother---Bob Russell, Bobby Scott

Hey Jude (BMI)---Lennon and McCartney

If He Walked Into My Life---Jerry Herman

If I Ruled the World---Leslie Bricusse, Cyril Ornadel

I Gotta Be Me---Walter Marks

I'll Catch the Sun---Rod McKuen

I'll Never Fall In Love Again---Burt Bacharach and Hal David

Impossible Dream, The   ---Joe Darion, Mitchell Leigh

I Say a Little Prayer---Burt Bacharach and Hal David

Is That All There Is?---Jerry Leiber, Mike Stoller

It Must Be Him---Mack David, Hilbert Becaud, Maurice Vidalin

It's Not Unusual (BMI)---Gordon Mills, Les Reed

It's Over---Jimmy Rodgers

It's Such a Pretty World Today---Dale Noe

It Was a Very Good Year---Ervin Drake

I Will Wait For You (BMI)---Michel Legrand, Norman Gimbel, Jacques Denez

Jean---Rod McKuen

Kind of a Hush---Les Reed, Geoff Stephens

King Of the Road (BMI)---Roger Miller

Lemon Tree---Will Hold

Leaving on a Jet Plane---John Denver

Let the Sunshine In---Galt MacDermot, James Rado, Gerome Ragni

Light My Fire---The Doors: J. Deusmore, R. Krieger, R. Manzaarek, J. Morrison

Like To Get To Know You---Stuart Scharf

Little Green Apples---Bobby Russell

Live For Life (BMI)---Francis Lai, Norman Gimbel

Look of Love, The ---Burt Bacharach and Hal David

Love Is Blue---Bryan Blackburn, Pierre Cour, Andre Popp
Love Me Tonight (BMI)---Barry Mason, D. Pace, Pilat, M. Panzeri
Loving You Has Made Me Bananas---Guy Marks
MacArthur Park---Jimmy Webb
Mame---Jerry Herman
Man and a Woman, A ---Pierre Barouch, Jerry Keller, Francis Lai
Michelle (BMI)---Lennon and McCartney
Midnight Cowboy---John Barry, Jacob Gold
Mrs. Robinson (BMI)---Paul Simon
Music To Watch Girls By---Sid Ramin, Tony Velona
My Cherie Amour (BMI)---Henry Cosby, Sylvia Moy, Stevie Wonder
My Way (BMI)---Paul Anka, Jacques Revaux, Claude Francois
Never My Love (BMI)---Donald & Richard Addrisi
Ob-La-Di--Ob-La-Da---Lennon and McCartney
Odd Couple, The ---Sammy Cahn, Neal Hefti
Ode To Billy Joe, The ---Bobby Gentry
On a Clear Day---Burton Lane, Alan Jay Lerner
On the South Side Of Chicago---Phil Zeller
Pass Me By---Cy Coleman, Carolyn Leigh
Promises Promises---Burt Bacharach and Hal David
Proud Mary (BMI)---John C. Fogerty
Raindrops Keep Falling On My Head---Burt Bacharach and Hal David
Romeo and Juliet love theme (A time for us) ---L. Kusik, Nino Rota, E. Snyder
Scarborough Fair (BMI)---Traditional, Paul Simon and Art Garfunkel
Seattle---Jake Keller, Hugh Montenegro, Ernie Sheldon
See You In September---Sherman Edwards, Sid Wayne
Shadow Of Your Smile, The ---Johnny Mandel, Paul F. Webster
She---Charles Aznavour, Charles Kretzner
Sherry---James Lipton, Lawrence Rosenthal
She Touched Me---Milton Shafer, Ira Levin
Something Stupid (BMI)---C. Carson Parks
Somewhere My Love (Lara's theme)---Maurice Jarre, Paul F. Webster
Sound of Silence, The (BMI)---Paul Simon
Spanish Eyes (BMI)---Bert Kaempfert, Eddie Snyder, Charles Singleton
Spooky (BMI)---Harry Middlebrooks, Mike Shapiro
Stand By Your Man (BMI)---Tammy Wynette, Billy Sherrill
Star! ---Sammy Cahn, James Van Heusen
Step To the Rear---Elmer Bernstein, Carolyn Leigh
Straight Life (BMI)---Sonny Curtis
Strangers In the Night (BMI)---Bert Kaempfert, Eddie Snyder, Charles Singleton
Summer Samba (BMI)---Norman Gimbel, Marcus Valle, Paulo Sergio Valle
Summer Wind, The ---Hans Bradke---Johnny Mercer, Henry Mayer
Sunny (BMI)---Bobby Hebb
Sunrise-Sunset (BMI)---Sheldon Harnick, Jerry Bock
Sunshine, Lollipops and Rainbows---Marvin Hamlisch, Howard Liebling
Sweetheart Tree, The ---Henry Mancini, Johnny Mercer
Talk To the Animals (BMI)---Leslie Bricusse
This Guy's In Love With You---Burt Bacharach and Hal David
This Is My Song---Charlie Chaplin
Thoroughly Modern Millie---Sammy Cahn, James Van Heusen
Those Were the Days---Gene Raskin
Time For Love, A (Romeo and Juliet film)---By L. Kusik, Nino Rota, E. Schneider
Tiny Bubbles---Leon Pober
To Sir With Love (BMI)---Don Black, Mark London
Traces (BMI) --- Buddy Buie, Emory Gordy, James B. Cobb, Jr.
True Grit---Elmer Bernstein, Don Black
Turn - Turn - Turn (BMI)---Pete Seeger
Up - Up and Away (BMI)---Jimmy Webb
Valley Of the Dolls---Andre Previn, Dory Langdon Previn
Walking Happy---Sammy Cahn, James Van Heusen

Walk In the Black Forest, A (BMI)---Horst Jankowski
What Did I Have That I Don't Have---Burton Lane, Alan Jay Lerner
What Now My Love?---Pierre Delanoe, Carl Sigman, Gilbert Becaud
What the World Needs Now Is Love---Burt Bacharach, Hal David
What's New, Pussycat?---Burt Bacharach, Hal David
Where Am I Going?---Cy Coleman, Dorothy Fields
Winchester Cathedral---Geoff Stephens
Windmills Of Your Mind, The ---Alan and Marilyn Bergman, Michel Legrand
Wichita Lineman, The ---Jimmy Webb
Wish Me a Rainbow---Ray Evans, Jay Livingston
Wonderful, Wonderful---Sherman Edwards, Ben Raleigh
Yellow Days--- A. Careillo, A. Bernstein
Yellow Submarine (BMI)---Lennon and McCartney
Yesterday (BMI)---Lennon and McCartney
Yesterday, When I Was Young---Charles Aznavour, Herbert Kretzmer
Yester-me, Yester-you, Yesterday---Ronald Miller, Bryan Wells
You Only Live Twice (BMI)---Leslie Bricusse, John Barry
You're Gonna Hear From Me -- Andre Previn, Dory Langdon Previn

1970-1974
Ain't No Sunshine (BMI)---Bill Withers
Alone Again, Naturally (BMI)---Gilbert O'Sullivan
American Pie (BMI)---Don McLean
And I Love You So (BMI)---Don McLean
Annie's Song---John Denver
Applause---Lee Adams, Charles Strouse
All In Love Is Fair---Stevie Wonder
Baby, Don't Get Hooked On Me (BMI)---Mac Davis
Bad - Bad Leroy Brown---Jim Croce
Before the Parade Passes By---Lee Adams, Jerry Herman, Charles Strouse
Behind Locked Doors (BMI)---Kenny O'Dell
Ben---Donald Black, Walter Scharf
Bless the Beasts and the Children---Barry DeVorzen, Pierre Botkin
Brian's Song---Michel Legrand, Alan & Marilyn Bergman
Bridge Over Troubled Waters (BMI)---Paul Simon
Candy Man, The (BMI)---Anthony Newley, Leslie Bricusse
Cecelia (BMI)---Paul Simon
Clair---Gilbert O'Sullivan
Daddy, Don't You Walk So Fast---Peter Robin Callander, Geoff Stephens
Day After Day---William Peter Ham
Day By Day---Stephen Schwartz
Delta Dawn---Alex Harvey, Larry Collins
Dueling Banjos (BMI)---Arthur Smith
Everything Is Beautiful (BMI)---Ray Stevens
Feelings---Morris Albert (lost a plagiarism suit)
Fire and Rain (BMI)---James Taylor
First Time Ever I Saw Your Face, The (BMI)---Ewan MacColl
Follow Me---John Denver
For All We Know (BMI)---Fred Karlin, Robb Royer, James Griffin
For the Good Times (BMI)---Kris Kristofferson
Goodbye To Love---John Bettis, Richard Carpenter
Help Me Make It Through the Night---Kris Kristofferson
Holly Holy---Neil Diamond
Hurting Each Other---Gary Geld, Peter Udell
I Am, I Said---Neil Diamond
I Am Woman (BMI)---Helen Reddy, Ray Burton
I Believe In Music (BMI)---Mac Davis
I Can See Clearly Now---Johnny Nash
I'd Like To Teach the World To Sing---W. Backer, R. Cook, R. Davis, R. Greenaway
I Don't Know How To Love Him---Timothy Rice, Andrew L. Webber

If---David Gates
If You Could Read My Mind---Gordon Lightfoot
I'll Be There---Berry Gordy Jr., Bobbie West, Willie Hutch, Hal Davis
I'll Have To Say I Love You In a Song---Jim Croce
Instant Karma --- John Lennon
It Never Rains In Southern California---Michael Hazelwood, Albert Hammond
It's Impossible---Canche Manzanero, Sid Wayne
I Want You Back --- Berry Gordy Jr., Freddie Perren, Al Mizell, Deke Richards
Joy To the World (BMI)---Hoyt Axton
Killing Me Softly With His Song (BMI)---Norman Gimbel, Charles Fox
Knock Three Times (BMI)---Irwin Levine, L. Russell Brown
Laughter In the Rain (BMI)---Neil Sedaka
Let It Be (BMI)---Lennon and McCartney
Life Is What You Make It---Marvin Hamlisch, Johnny Mercer
Little Prince, The ---Lerner and Loewe
Live and Let Die---Paul and Linda McCartney
Long and Winding Road, The (BMI)---Lennon and McCartney
Lord's Prayer, The ---Arnold Strals, Sister Janet Meade
Love Is All Around (M. Tylor Moore show) (BMI)---Reg Presley
Love's Theme---Barry White
Make It With You---David Gates
Midnight At the Oasis---David Nichtern
Morning After, The---Al Kasha, Joel Hirshhorn (BMI)
Most Beautiful Girl, The (BMI)---Norro Wilson, Billy Sherrill, Rory Bourke
Mr. Bojangles (BMI)---Jerry Jeff Walker
Music From Across the Way---James Last, Carl Sigman
My Guy---Smokey Robinson
My Love---Paul and Linda McCartney
My Sweet Lord (BMI)---George Harrison
Nadia's Theme --- Barry DeVorzon, Perry Botkin Jr.
Never Can Say Goodbye (BMI)---Clifton Davis
Never My Love --- Don and Dick Adddrisi
Night They Drove Old Dixie Down, The ---Jamie Robbie Robertson
Oh Babe, What Would You Say? ---E. S. Smith
Old Fashioned Love Song---Paul Williams
Old Fashioned Way, The ---Charles Aznavour, George Garvarevitz
One Less Bell To Answer---Burt Bacharach, Hal David
Pieces Of Dreams---Michel Legrand, Alan and Marilyn Bergman
Precious and Few---Walter Nims
Put Your Hand In the Hand (BMI)---Gene MacLellan
Rainy Days and Mondays---Roger Nichols and Paul Williams
Rose Garden (I Never Promised You a) (BMI)---Joe South
Save the Last Dance For Me (BMI)---Doc Pomus, Mort Schuman
Seasons In the Sun---Jacques Brel, Rod McKuen
Send In the Clowns---Stephen Sondheim
Sing---Joe Raposo
Snowbird (BMI)---Gene MacLellan
Song Sung Blue---Neil Diamond
Speak Softly, Love (Godfather theme)---Larry Kusik, Rinaldi Rota
Spirit In the Sky --- Norman Greenbaum
Suicide is Painless (Mash theme)---John Mandel, Mike Altman
Summer Knows, The ---Michel Legrand, Alan and Marilyn Bergman
Sunshine On My Shoulders---John Denver, Richard Kniss, Michael Taylor
Sweet Caroline---Neil Diamond
Take Me Home, Country Roads---Bill Danoff, John Denver, Taffy Nivert
They Long To Be Close To You---Burt Bacharach and Hal David
This Masquerade---Leon Russe
Tie a Yellow Ribbon Round the Old Oak Tree (BMI)---Irwine Livine, L. Russell Brown
Top Of the World---John Bettis, Richard Carpenter
Touch Me In the Morning---Michael Masser, Ron Miller

United We Stand---Tony Hiller, Peter Simons
Watchin' Scotty Grow (BNI)---Mac Davis
Way We Were, The ---Marvin Hamlisch, Alan and Marilyn Bergman
We May Never Love Like This Again---Al Kasha, Joel Hirshhorn (BMI)
We've Only Just Begun (BMI)---Paul Williams, Roger Nichols
What Are You Doing the Rest Of Your Life? ---Michel Legrand, A. & M. Bergman
What Have They Done To My Song, Ma? ---Melanie Safka
When You're Hot, You're Hot---Jerry Reed
Where Do I Begin (Love Story theme)---Francis Lai, Carl Sigman
Where Is the Love? ---Ralph MacDonald, William Salter
Whistling Away the Dark---Henry Mancini, Johnny Mercer
Winds of Chance, The (Airport theme)---Alfred Newman, Paul F. Webster
Woodstock (BMI)---Joni Mitchell
Yesterday Once More---John Bettis, Richard Carpenter
You and Me Against the World---Kenneth Asher, Paul Williams
You Are the Sunshine Of My Life---Stevie Wonder
You Don't Mess Around With Jim---Jim Croce
You've Got a Friend---Carol King Larkey

1975-1979
Behind Closed Doors---Kenny O'Dell
Blue Bayou---Joe Milson, Roy Orbison
Can't Smile Without You---Chris Arnold, David Martin, Geoff Marrow
Come In From the Rain---Melissa Manchester, Carol Bayer Sager
Copacabana (At the Copa)---Barry Manilow, Bruce Sussman, Jack Feldman
Deja Vu---Isaac Hayes, Adrienne Anderson
Don't Cry For Me, Argentina---Andrew Lloyd Webber,
Don't It Make My Brown Eyes Blue? ---Richard C. Leigh
Do You Know Where You're Going To---Michael Masser
Evergreen---Barbra Streisand, Paul Williams
Fame---Carlos Alomar, David Bowie
For the Good Times---Kris Kristofferson
Gonna Fly Now (From Rocky)---Carol Conors, Ayn Robbins
Help Me Make It Through the Night---Kris Kristofferson
How Lucky Can You Get? ---John Kander and Frederick Ebbs
I Could Be Happy With You---Julie Andrews, Sandy Wilson
I'll Catch the Sun and Never Give It Back Again---Rod McKuen
I'm Easy---Keith Carradine
It's Too Late---Carol King Larkey, Toni Stern
I Write the Songs---Bruce Arthur Johnston
Just the Way You Are---Billy Joel
Last Dance, The---Paul Jabara
Love Will Keep Us Together---Neil Sedaka
Laughter In the Rain---Neil Sedaka, Phil Cody
Make the World Go Away---Hank Cochran
Most Beautiful Girl, The ---Rory Bowke, Billy Shirill, Norm Wilson
My Cherie Amour---Henry Cosby, Stevie Wonder
Nobody Does It Better---Marvin Hamlisch, Carol Bayer Sager
Only Yesterday---John Bettis, Richard Carpenter
Rainy Day People---Gordon Lightfoot
Rhinestone Cowboy---Larry Weiss
Southern Nights---Allen Toussaint
Top Of the World---John Bettis, Richard Carpenter
Tie a Yellow Ribbon---Irwin Levine, L. Russell Brown
Tomorrow--Martin Charnin, Charles Strouse
What I Did For Love---Marvin Hamlisch and a BMI writer
With You, I'm Born Again---Lionel Richie
You Are So Beautiful---Bruce Fisher and a BMI writer
You Don't Bring Me Flowers Any More---Neil Diamond, Marilyn and Alan Bergman
You Light Up My Life---Joe Brooks

SONG INDEX

PERSONNEL INDEX